Who Pays
for Universal
Service?

Who Pays for Universal Service?

When Telephone Subsidies Become Transparent

Robert W. Crandall
Leonard Waverman

BROOKINGS INSTITUTION PRESS
Washington, D.C.

Copyright © 2000
BROOKINGS INSTITUTION
1775 Massachusetts Avenue, N.W.
Washington, D.C. 20036
www.brookings.edu

Library of Congress Cataloging-in-Publication data

Crandall, Robert W.
  Who pays for universal service? : when telephone subsidies become transparent / Robert W. Crandall and Leonard Waverman.
  p. cm.
  Includes bibliographical references and index.

  ISBN 0-8157-1612-5 (alk. paper)
  ISBN 0-8157-1611-7 (pbk. : alk. paper)
  1. Telecommunication policy-United States.   2. Telecommunications-Taxation-United States.   3. Telephone-United States.   I. Waverman, Leonard.   II. Title.
  HE7781 .C673 2000   99-050588
  384.6'3—dc21   CIP

9 8 7 6 5 4 3 2 1

The paper used in this publication meets minimum requirements of the American National Standard for Information Sciences—Permanence of Paper for Printed Library Materials: ANSI Z39.48-1984.

Typeset in Adobe Garamond

Composition by Northeastern Graphic Services
Hackensack, New Jersey

Printed by R. R. Donnelley and Sons
Harrisonburg, Virginia

₿ THE BROOKINGS INSTITUTION

The Brookings Institution is an independent organization devoted to nonpartisan research, education, and publication in economics, government, foreign policy, and the social sciences generally. Its principal purposes are to aid in the development of sound public policies and to promote public understanding of issues of national importance.

The Institution was founded on December 8, 1927, to merge the activities of the Institute for Government Research, founded in 1916, the Institute of Economics, founded in 1922, and the Robert Brookings Graduate School of Economics and Government, founded in 1924.

The general administration of the Institution is the responsibility of a Board of Trustees charged with safeguarding the independence of the staff and fostering the most favorable conditions for scientific research and publication. The immediate direction of the policies, program, and staff is vested in the president, assisted by an advisory committee of the officers and staff.

In publishing a study, the Institution presents it as a competent treatment of a subject worthy of public consideration. The interpretations or conclusions in such publications are those of the author or authors and do not necessarily reflect the views of the other staff members, officers, or trustees of the Brookings Institution.

Foreword

In the United States, and in virtually every other developed country, the telecommunications sector is being opened to competition. As new entrants appear, the ability of regulators to set prices to achieve political or social objectives declines. Keeping local rates low for residential subscribers, particularly those in rural areas, in the name of providing "universal service" and paying for the shortfall from excessive prices for other services, such as long-distance service, cannot be sustained in the face of competitive entry.

Robert W. Crandall and Leonard Waverman show that such universal policies are inefficient and unnecessary. They argue that there is no need to keep residential rates low in developed countries, because virtually everyone would subscribe to telephone service at cost-based, competitive rates in any case. Nor is there any basis for keeping these rates low for low-income households, given that the local telephone bill is such a small share of even the poorest families' budgets. Ironically, traditional universal service policies often hurt many of the telephone subscribers they are supposed to help, namely, rural subscribers who use their telephones intensively. Eliminating the subsidies implicit in current U.S. universal service policy would result in gains to the economy of as much as $7 billion a year.

The concept of universal service is not disappearing from the U.S. regulators' lexicon, however, but is actually being extended to new services, such as Internet connections for schools and libraries and below-cost connections for rural health facilities. These new universal service subsidies are being paid for by a tax on interstate long-distance services. Crandall and Waverman question whether such targeted subsidies are good educational or social policy: Why should telecommunications services be treated differently from school books, teachers, or desks? Moreover, taxing interstate long-distance service to support these subsidies is much more costly to the economy than using general tax revenues for that purpose.

The authors are indebted to Peyton Wynns, Bill Rogerson, Evan Kwerel, Melvyn Fuss, Clifford Winston, James Eisner, and their colleagues in seminar presentations at the Brookings Institution and the London Business School for helpful comments and suggestions. They also thank Lynn Lin, Kathleen Withers, and Patricia Powers for their valuable research assistance and Jennifer Eichberger for her untiring efforts in both research assistance and verification of the manuscript. Theresa Walker and Tanjam Jacobson edited the manuscript; Carlotta Ribar proofread and Sherry Smith indexed the pages. The authors are indebted to the Markle Foundation, Bell Atlantic, Mastercard International, and Sprint for financial support of this research and to PNR, Inc., and Statistics Canada for data.

The views expressed here are solely those of the authors and should not be ascribed to any of the persons or institutions acknowledged above or to the trustees, officers, or other staff members of the Brookings Institution.

MICHAEL H. ARMACOST
President

May 2000
Washington, D.C.

Contents

ix

Tables

Figures

Who Pays
for Universal
Service?

1 | Universal Service and Telecommunications Policy

The telecommunications sectors in most advanced countries are being buffeted by major changes. Once a set of tranquil government-owned monopolies, these sectors are being transformed into competitive industries. In the United States, the 1996 Telecommunications Act has been designed to open the markets for local telephone services to competition and to allow the regional Bell operating companies (RBOCs) to enter the long-distance market. In Canada, all telecommunications markets have been opened to competition. In Europe, the United Kingdom privatized its telephone monopoly in 1984 and then began opening the market to competition. Denmark and Finland followed in the 1990s, and all voice telephone services in twelve of the fifteen European Union countries were opened fully to competitive entry on January 1, 1998.

Elsewhere, government-owned telephone companies are being privatized and confronted with the threat of entry from new competitors, forcing these erstwhile monopolies to improve service, become more efficient, and therefore reduce employment. Independent regulatory authorities are replacing government postal, telephone, and telegraph (PTT) ministries as authorities that control telephone rates and services. This liberalization is occurring in diverse countries, such as Chile, Hong Kong, and Singapore.

1

The electromagnetic spectrum is being auctioned off to new mobile service operators in Brazil, South Africa, the Netherlands, the United Kingdom, and a number of others. Pressures from new entry will only intensify in the wake of the World Trade Organization (WTO) agreement on services, in which sixty-nine countries agreed to open their telecommunications market to competition, allow some degree of foreign ownership, and abide by open and transparent regulatory regimes.[1] Equally important, the United States is leading a charge to reduce international telephone rates from their current stratospheric levels.[2] These reductions in international rates will severely reduce the ability of national telecommunications carriers to use international services to support a variety of other services.

"Universal Service"

All of these decisions have much to commend them. Developing and developed economies require a healthy, dynamic telecommunications sector if they are to prosper in an increasingly global economy.[3] But moving from public monopoly to private monopoly and ultimately to a relatively competitive telecommunications sector places strains on various government policies that were essentially hidden from public view for decades. The most obvious of these is the level of employment in the telecommunications sector, but an even more sensitive problem in most countries is cloaked in the concept of "universal service"—keeping monthly charges for residential service below incremental cost and making up the difference by allowing carriers to charge very high prices for long distance and other services. These policies are justified as necessary to ensure that virtually all residences are connected to the telephone network. If liberalization results in an end to such transfers and, therefore, higher residential charges for renting a local telephone line, some critics fear that many low-income and rural residences will simply disconnect their service even though recent studies of the residential demand for telephone service cast substantial doubt on such predictions.[4]

The incredible pace of technical change in communications is even adding new dimensions to the political demand for universal service. Access to simple voice telephony is no longer enough in some countries. Advocates of universal service are now pressing for policies to provide consumers or public institutions, such as schools and libraries, with advanced, high-speed telecommunications services at prices below the costs of these services. In the United States, for example, the 1996 Telecommunications Act that is supposed to open telecom markets to competition also requires regulators to add new universal service obligations for libraries, schools, and rural medical facilities to the existing residential voice-service requirements. These new obligations complicate the process of substituting competition for regulated monopoly and greatly increase the burden on other telecommunications services.

No one has carefully estimated the costs and benefits of the traditional or the new universal service obligations or carefully identified the recipients and sources of the subsidies—the gainers and losers. In this book, we analyze the demand for residential telephone service, calling patterns, and telephone expenditures across a variety of developed countries, with detailed data for the United States, Canada, and the United Kingdom. In so doing, we develop an estimate of the social cost of universal service policies for the United States while considering the U.S. requirements in an international perspective.

Two Definitions of Universal Service

This book examines public policies in the telecommunications sector, concentrating on the prices set for access to the telecom network and the prices for various types of calling. A decade or two ago, such a work would be focused on ordinary voice telephone service. Universality of telephone service in this older environment would simply imply that telephone service be available to everyone, that is, that the cost of connecting to the network, including free inward calls, and perhaps initiating a certain number of outbound calls, be affordable to citizens of all incomes. This version of universal service essentially turns on the definition of "affordable," particularly in wealthy countries where the cost of modern telephone service is an extremely small share of even low-income household budgets.[5] Affordability of basic telephone service in these countries is often related to the ability of certain individuals or families to limit their discretionary expenditures on national or international calls that are difficult to predict and, in some cases, to control. If these households are unable to control their use of such services, they discover that they are unable to pay their monthly telephone bills—of which the monthly cost of access may be but a small share—and therefore risk having their basic telephone service terminated because of unpaid long-distance charges.

Universal service has recently come to have another meaning: the availability of new, innovative services to all potential users. This concept of universal service has implications for national competition policy and for rate regulation. The narrowest version of this policy requires that all subscribers have access to new services, whether provided by their basic telephone service provider or by other companies. To facilitate access to these new services, many countries have begun to require that basic telephone companies interconnect with all other companies providing basic or enhanced telecommunications services. The rules and rates for such interconnection are at the center of the debate over how to admit competition in telecommunications in most countries in the Organization for Economic Cooperation and Development (OECD) today.

This second definition of universal service may be extended to the promotion of new services through prices that are below the network provider's average cost, or even its marginal cost, because of network externalities. The development of e-mail provides an excellent example of the case for such pricing: one person's decision to subscribe to an e-mail service increases the value of e-mail to all others who may communicate with that person. This externality provides a rationale for subsidizing the access to e-mail if, at the margin, the benefits to others from additional subscribers exceed the cost of the subsidy.[6] Unfortunately, it is difficult to know which of a large potential number of new services may be worth subsidizing through below-cost pricing. The existence of network externalities is not a sufficient condition for a public (or private) policy of subsidizing a new service.[7]

In the United States, the concept of universal service has now been extended to the provision of new, high-speed telecom services to public institutions, such as schools, libraries, and medical facilities.[8] The aid to schools and libraries is for Internet access, and the assistance to rural medical facilities is to reduce their telecommunications charges to the level paid by urban health providers. Under this new universal service policy, not only poor and rural residences but now thousands of public institutions are to be the recipients of intraindustry subsidies—to be provided by a large indirect (excise) tax on all telecommunications service providers. These new taxes may not thwart liberalization, but they are surely an impediment to deregulation and to moving telecom rates toward cost.

Is the universal service justification for subsidizing households, services, or institutions unique to telecommunications? Why does it not exist for other services, such as housing, electricity, or heating?[9] Both the refrigerator and the television set are ubiquitous across the United States and other countries. In fact, their penetration rate (the percentage of households having the durable) is above that for telephones. Even in many poorer countries, TV penetration exceeds telephone penetration. Television sets, refrigerators, VCRs, and washing machines are often more expensive for users to buy and even perhaps to operate than telephones and have not been promoted or subsidized as critical "universal" services. Yet refrigerators, for example, surely generate positive externalities through keeping food from perishing, thus reducing the spread of disease. Even television may generate externalities—the ability to be informed or to be made aware of cultural values and icons.[10]

Why is it that these other goods have household penetration rates approaching or exceeding that of telephones without any "universal service" program? Or put another way, is the universal service objective for telephony a euphemism for policies that have little to do with universality but were developed—as some have suggested—to prevent competitive entry, and are these practices now a significant barrier to competition?[11] Moreover, is the extension of intraindustry subsidies to Internet access for schools and libraries necessary, and would alternative sources of such funding—such as general tax revenues—not be a more efficient method of funding these needs?

The Origins of Universal Service Policy in the United States

The U.S. telephone industry did not begin as a natural monopoly. Indeed, the source of monopoly in early telephony was not the nature of the distribution system, or network, but patents owned by the Bell Company.[12] Once the last of these patents expired in 1894, the U.S. telephone industry began to be buffeted by entry into local services. Local rates began to fall, often sharply, in response to this entry. Price wars were common. Disputes over interconnection of competing networks became commonplace.[13]

Even after Bell's patents for the basic telephone expired, it had newer patents on long-distance service. Non-Bell operating companies were routinely denied access to the Bell long-distance network, prompting many complaints. However, as Milton Mueller points out, this refusal to interconnect was symmetrical—the new independent telephone companies at the turn of the century did not want to have to interconnect with the local Bell companies either.[14] By the end of the first decade of the twentieth century, there were as many independent exchanges as Bell exchanges; most cities had at least two competing telephone companies; and nearly half of all subscribers were connected to independent companies that did not interconnect with the Bell network.[15]

This fragmented structure of the early telephone industry gave rise to the first utterances of "universal service." Mueller attributes the first use of the phrase to Theodore Vail, writing in AT&T's *1907 Annual Report.* Universal service was seen by Vail as the delivery of all telephone service through one "system," guided by one "policy."[16] Obviously, he saw universal service as requiring a nationally integrated single system, managed by AT&T. During the next few years, AT&T would expand its local exchanges dramatically while also purchasing many of its independent competitors. This activity, and the incessant rate wars between AT&T and the independents, attracted the interest of the antitrust authorities. As a result, Vail could only move AT&T toward his goal of a single, integrated national telephone company by accepting government regulation.

The 1913 Kingsbury Commitment, an agreement between AT&T and the Justice Department, ended much of this controversy. The Justice Department would drop its antitrust investigation of AT&T in return for AT&T's agreement to sell its interest in Western Electric; cease its acquisitions of independent companies; and interconnect its long-distance network to the independent companies. Eight years later, however, AT&T's acquisitions were to begin anew in response to the Willis-Graham Act of 1921 that immunized them from antitrust attack. Within a few years, AT&T would acquire many independent companies, leaving only about 20 percent of the country's local exchange service in the hands of non-Bell companies.

This drive toward universality was the first incarnation of a "universal service" policy—a single, unified local and long-distance service in the hands of a regulated AT&T. Vail largely succeeded in achieving this goal, but it was a very different goal from that understood as "universal service" today. There was no deliberate policy of underpricing local residential connections by overpricing long-distance calls.[17] Businesses were not to be charged more for local connections than were residences. Indeed, on the eve of the Willis-Graham Act, the federal government's seminal pronouncement in favor of Vail's vision, only 35 percent of households had a telephone. Universal service did not mean that access to a telephone was universal in 1920, only that the telephone network was moving toward consolidation in AT&T's universe.

The Origins of the New "Universal Service" Policy in the United States

For the past quarter century, more than 90 percent of U.S. households have had a telephone, and most of the remaining households are likely to have had relatively easy access to one. Telephone penetration—the share of households connected to the telephone network—grew steadily from the bottom of the 1930s Depression, almost doubling between 1935 and 1950 from about 32 percent to 62 percent.[18] Yet this was a period in which there was little discussion of universal telephone service. Rather, regulators struggled with the formula to be used in apportioning the fixed (non-traffic-sensitive) costs of the telephone network between interstate and intrastate services for the purposes of establishing telephone rates. It was not until 1947 that regulators finally settled on a separations policy that divided these costs between the two jurisdictions, and the first rates based on this separation of costs were only filed in 1950. At that time only 3 percent of the non-traffic-sensitive, local-network costs were apportioned to the interstate jurisdiction, but this represented the first attempt to shift some of the fixed costs of connecting subscribers to the price of interstate calls.[19]

Another twenty-five years elapsed before the modern definition of universal service emerged—once again tendered by an AT&T that faced dire trouble. In 1974 the Department of Justice filed a massive Sherman Act case against AT&T, proposing to break AT&T into several companies to ameliorate its monopoly power. In response to this threat, AT&T hired Eugene V. Rostow (who had chaired President Lyndon Johnson's 1968 Task Force on Communications Policy) to testify before Congress in 1975 on the threats to AT&T's "universal and optimized" telephone network. Apparently, this was the first time AT&T had revived the notion of universal service, albeit a new definition. Universal no longer meant that all subscribers, whether they totaled 25, 30, or 60 percent of households, subscribed to the same network. Now universal service meant that the telephone was truly ubiquitous, that everyone—or nearly everyone—enjoyed access to plain old telephone service, regardless of the supplier.

The change in the definition of universal service was necessary because AT&T was confronted by a new kind of competition that developed out of the unfortunate politics of regulation. After 1950, the joint federal-state board that divided the non-traffic-sensitive costs of the local network between "state" and "interstate" jurisdictions moved an increasing share of these costs into the federal jurisdiction. By the mid-1970s, 20 percent of these costs were assigned to interstate calls through this artifice even though such costs did not vary with minutes of calling in any jurisdiction. Quite simply, this was a "cross-subsidy" in the popular sense from interstate long-distance calls to local service. At the same time, state regulators allowed the price of local business connections to be set far above the rates for residential connections. They also generally permitted all local urban rates—both business and residential—to be substantially above rural rates even though the relative costs of service would have required precisely the opposite.[20]

These rate distortions began to invite a new kind of competition, not from independent local companies as was the case at the turn of the century, but at first from competitive long-distance carriers and later from local urban carriers (now known as CAPs, or competitive access providers).[21] These entrants were clearly attracted by the prospects of arbitrage possibilities created by politically minded regulators. In 1969 Microwave Communications, Inc. (MCI) was granted a license by the Federal Communications Commission (FCC) to offer limited, private-line interstate service for business customers.[22] In 1971 the FCC opened this private-line market to general entry, but it was not until 1974 that MCI began to offer its business customers a standard switched long-distance service that could connect with any U.S. telephone subscriber. This new service was not expressly authorized by the FCC, but MCI offered it anyway and survived attempts by the FCC to enforce an order in the courts to discontinue the service.

MCI's competition in long-distance services exposed AT&T's source of support for below-cost residential service to competitive attack. At this point, AT&T could have begun a long struggle to reverse the regulators' unfortunate decisions to assign so much of the non-traffic-sensitive costs of its local networks to interstate long distance, or it could have attempted to fight off competition by frustrating MCI's and others' attempts to interconnect with its network while seeking legislation to limit the role of competition. It chose the latter course; hence, Rostow's invocation of the new "universal service" proposal. The rate distortions had to be perpetuated to keep local service rates artificially low and thus "affordable" for millions of Americans, but AT&T needed relief from competition and antitrust to carry out this policy.

Obviously, AT&T lost this battle, but it won the war of the words. This new definition of universal service has achieved a prominent role in the regulators' and politicians' lexicon—that of defending a rate structure that cannot be defended on pure economic grounds[23] and that cannot withstand the onslaught of competition unless formalized in a system of long-distance access charges. The new long-distance competitors had to be charged their "fair share" of the cost of the local connections. The FCC and the states thus moved from an implicit decision to keep long-distance rates high through regulatory accounting of costs to a formal system of above-cost access charges that long-distance companies pay local-exchange companies to connect their calls.

When AT&T was subsequently broken up through a consent decree that settled the government's 1974 antitrust case against it, the average interstate access charge was more than seventeen cents a minute.[24] Today it is about three cents a minute and falling, but the per minute charge is still far above the long-run incremental costs of connecting a call.[25] Intrastate access charges are even higher. This implicit support of local telephone service from long-distance services continues, as do the implicit transfers to local rural connections that are still embedded in the regulated rate structures.

The Shift to Explicit Universal Service Subsidies in the United States

Besides the implicit transfers and even "subsidies" embedded in the U.S. telephone rate structure, there are also direct subsidies paid directly from "universal service funds" to local telephone companies to fund reduced rates for low-income subscribers and to compensate local companies for high-cost operations.[26] These funds are raised principally from a charge on long-distance companies.

The first of these programs, Lifeline, is a federal-state subsidy program designed by the FCC in 1984 and 1985 to reduce the monthly subscription rate for qualifying low-income households. The federal portion had been funded from revenues collected from long-distance carriers on the basis of each carrier's presubscribed lines.[27] The amount of the subsidy had been up to twice the federal subscriber line charge, or a maximum of $7 a month, with intrastate carrier operations funding half the cost.[28] In 1987 the FCC supplemented the Lifeline program with a Link-Up America program, designed to subsidize the installation charge for qualifying low-income households. This latter program pays one-half of the initial installation charges up to a maximum of $30 and subsidizes the interest charges on deferred payment programs of up to twelve months for up to $200 of these connection charges. The cost of the federal portion of these two programs in 1998 was $464 million, or about $2.67 a year for each access line (table 1-1). This was equivalent to 13.4 percent of the average residential rate.

Table 1-1. *The Cost of Federal Universal Service Programs, 1998*

Program	Annual cost ($ millions)	Annual cost per local carrier line ($)[a]
Lifeline	422	2.43
Link-Up	42	.24
High-cost support	827	4.75
Long-term support	472	2.71
Switching costs	413	2.37
Total	2,176	12.52

Sources: Federal Communications Commission (FCC), "Trends in Telephone Service" (1999), tables 1, 8.3, 8.5, 22.1, 22.2.

a. Annual cost divided by total Universal Service Fund loops.

In addition, the FCC has subsidized a substantial share of the costs of local exchange companies in high-cost areas. This "high-cost assistance" program has also been funded from long-distance carriers in a complicated manner, and it has been far more expensive than the Lifeline and Link-Up programs combined. A Universal Service Fund (USF) was established through a tax on presubscribed long-distance lines to fund high-cost connections (local loops) to subscribers through a complicated formula. In 1998 this fund distributed $827 million to high-cost (that is, rural) local telephone carriers through a charge of nearly $5.00 per presubscribed long-distance access line. Local telephone companies have contributed annually to a fund to cross-subsidize high-cost companies even further through a "long-term support" program. In 1998 these payments totaled $472 million or nearly $3.00 a year per local line for the companies who provided the subsidy. Finally, there has been a program to fund high-cost companies' allegedly high switching costs through a levy on the interstate access charges that are paid by long-distance carriers to originate and terminate their calls. This subsidy totaled $413 million in 1998. Thus, the direct high-cost subsidies paid directly to rural, high-cost companies ($1.712 billion in 1998) have been much more costly than the direct subsidies ($464 million in 1998) targeted on low-income subscribers. All of these programs were supported by what is, in effect, a tax of 3 percent on interstate telecommunications services.[29]

The incentive effects of the high-cost fund are likely to be substantially adverse to economic efficiency, given that a "high-cost" carrier is generally reimbursed in proportion to its costs. For instance, under the high-cost program the share of the fixed, non-traffic-sensitive costs reimbursed rose from 0 percent for areas whose costs were less than 15 percent above the national average to 75 percent of the costs for areas whose non-traffic-sensitive costs exceeded 150 percent of the national average. Moreover, the focus of the tax to support these payments on interstate carriers' presubscribed lines provided an incentive for inefficient substitution of private lines, resellers, or call-by-call services for a preselected carrier.

Under the 1996 Telecommunications Act, most of these federal high-cost support programs are being replaced by a direct subsidy program that is to be based on the difference between the Federal Communications Commission's estimate of forward-looking costs and a "benchmark" estimate of a reasonable rate for local service. The support payments are to be explicit, portable, and paid for by a tax based on all interstate and international revenues.[30] Interstate access charges, the source of much of the support payments under the earlier regime, are to be reduced dollar for dollar by the new tax revenues, but the FCC decision to reduce these access charges was postponed until January 2000 while the commission settled on a final high-cost support policy.[31]

The FCC spent three years in a controversial process of calibrating its "model" of forward-looking costs for this program that was originally to begin in January 1999. In late 1999, the commission finally completed the process of establishing the high-cost support levels for nonrural carriers, having set interim levels for rural carriers in 1997. The total projected cost of these programs for 2000 will be $1.925 billion, requiring a tax on interstate and international revenues of 2.6 percent.[32] Although not required by FCC regulation or the 1996 Telecommunications Act, the replacement of indirect intrastate support of high-cost residential lines by a program similar to that enacted by the FCC is anticipated as local competition develops. Unfortunately, the federal subsidy program will remain complex and controversial in no small part because of the politics of redistributing revenues from low-cost to high-cost states and the jurisdictional rivalries inherent in the U.S. regulatory system.

The New (New) U.S. Concept of Universal Service

In a later chapter, we analyze the need to erect cross-subsidies to ensure virtual universality of subscription to telephone service in a country as advanced as the United States. But in the wake of the 1996 act, this is obviously too modest a task. The act not only enshrines the notion of maintaining artificially low monthly rates for local residential voice service, but it even extends this philosophy to new services while at the same time professing to promote competition. Now the FCC is to establish a new program of federal support from taxes on telecommunication carrier revenues to pay for advanced services to schools and libraries and to establish below-cost telephone rates for certain rural medical facilities. The act requires a joint board of federal and state regulators to provide guidance for establishing the support levels for these programs. This board issued its report in 1996,[33] and the commission subsequently voted to fund the schools and libraries program at $2.25 billion a year and rural medical facilities at $400 million a year.[34] In the ensuing three years, the program has been enmeshed in continuing controversy over the amount of funding, the definition of the revenue base from which the funds are to be raised, and the efficiency of the administration of the entire program. By the end of 1999, the FCC was spending approximately $2 billion a year on these programs, requiring a tax on interstate and international revenues of 3 percent.[35]

If Congress wished to vote for efficient, explicit subsidies for connecting high-cost residences, schools, libraries, or rural medical facilities, it could have funded such support from general revenues or from a relatively efficient tax.[36] By leaving the setting of the tax to federal regulators, Congress implicitly encouraged them to continue the policy of levying taxes on services with relatively high price elasticities of demand, thereby continuing the inefficient policies of the past. As we describe in a later chapter, these taxes on price-elastic services cost society much more lost output than do taxes on less price-elastic services, such as basic connections to the network. These inefficiencies are likely to be magnified by the growth in the types of services to be supported. Thus, the newest universal service policy is likely to resemble the older policy in a new disguise—and one with far more services to support.

Other Countries

The United States is not alone in promoting universal service in telecommunications policy, but the complexity of its state and federal policies is unique. Other OECD countries are now actively debating the role of regulated rates in ensuring universality of telephone service, particularly as they privatize their national carriers and open up their traditional telephone monopolies to competition. However, none is anticipating the myriad programs designed to subsidize high-cost operations or targeted facilities, such as schools, libraries, and medical establishments.

Canada

Although most telephone companies in Canada have always been private, Canada did not begin to liberalize its telephone sector until the mid-1980s. This liberalization was extremely limited before 1992 when the Canadian Radio-Television and Telecommunications Commission (CRTC) began to allow facilities-based competition. Subsequently, the passage of the 1993 Telecommunications Act clarified the CRTC's jurisdiction over all telecommunications regulation in Canada, and the CRTC moved aggressively to begin the liberalization of local telecommunications. But Canada entered this new era with a rate structure that was even more distorted than that of the United States.[37] This rate structure could not survive open entry and competition; therefore, the CRTC began to rebalance rates toward relative cost following its 1992 decision to open long-distance markets to competition.

The commission proposed to reduce "contributions" from long-distance to local exchange services by imposing a succession of three $2.00 a month local rate increases over the next three years.[38] This proposal was delayed by the intervention of the Cabinet but was essentially reinstated in 1995.[39] By the end of 1998, these increases would reduce the contribution from long-distance services to no more than two cents a minute.[40]

The CRTC thus essentially affirmed its historical policy of internal cross-subsidies or "contributions" from long-distance services to local residential rates, arguing that it must do so because competition cannot be relied on to keep all residential rates "affordable." This is in contrast with the United States, which is shifting to a more transparent tax on all telecommunications revenues to fund its interstate universal service requirement. But Canada is not extending its universal service policy to new services just yet; hence its universal service policy may turn out to be less onerous than those policies being established or perpetuated in the United States.

Europe

Because telecommunications liberalization only began in earnest on January 1, 1998, any discussion of universal service policy in European countries is likely to be overtaken by changing regulatory policies. It is important to stress, however, that most European countries differ greatly from the United States and Canada in the method of charging for local telephone service. The European countries do not offer flat-rate service; rather, they generally charge relatively low, geographically uniform monthly "line rental" rates with substantial local usage (per minute) rates that vary with the time of day. As a result, European subscribers use their telephones far less than Canadians or Americans. In 1994–95, for example, the average number of local calls per line in EU countries ranged from 760 to 1,170 a year compared with 3,000 calls a year in the United States.[41] Therefore, any analysis of European universal service subsidies for basic telephony must address the monthly line charge and the local usage rate.

As of 1996, most EU countries had universal service policies that extended solely to basic services (table 1-2). However, with liberalization being pushed by the European Commission through directives enforcing open networks and transparent, cost-based interconnection regimes, the commission has also introduced measures to prevent countries from using a universal service obligation to reduce competition. The commission states that universal service obligations can include geographic rate averaging for voice telephony, public phones, and public directories. The costs of the universal service obligations can be covered by a Universal Service Fund extracted from all operators.[42] Any access deficit—the imbalance between revenues from customer line rentals and their costs—is not part of the USF, but it may be recovered as a separate tax only until 2000. If other services are added to the universal service obligation, these cannot be charged for in a USF.[43]

Before the 1998 liberalization deadline, most EU countries had established their universal policies by statute, and most therefore had uniform ("affordable") local rates. Surprisingly, few offered low-user discounts although most required some form of discount for the disabled. As in the United States and Canada, all but three countries allowed the telecom operator to terminate service for nonpayment of bills.

Traditionally, the most important characteristic of European universal service policies has been the low and generally geographically uniform monthly charge for a residential line. Table 1-3 provides comparable data for most OECD countries, including the EU, Australia, New Zealand, the United States, and Canada. Most of the EU countries have uniform rates, but the United States and Canada do not. We delve into the cost of providing local service in a later chapter, but for now we note that residen-

Table 1-2. Universal Service Policies in the European Union, 1996

Country	Legal obligation	Services covered	Affordability criterion	Uniform national rates	Low-user discounts	Disability discounts	Disconnect for nonpayment
Austria	Yes	Basic	No	Yes	No	No	Yes
Belgium	Yes	Basic	Yes	No	No	Yes	No
Denmark	Yes	Basic plus ISDN	No	No	No	Yes	Yes
Finland	Yes	Basic	No	No	No	Yes	Yes
France	Yes	Basic	Yes	Yes	Yes	Yes	No
Germany	Yes	Basic, directory services, pay phones	Yes	Yes, but changing in 1998	No	Yes	Yes
Greece	No	None	Yes	No	No	Yes	Yes
Ireland	No	None	No	Yes	No	No	Yes
Italy	No	None	No	Yes	Yes	No	Yes
Luxembourg	No	None	No	Yes	No	Yes	Yes
Netherlands	Yes	Basic plus billing	No	Yes	No	Yes	Yes
Portugal	Yes	Basic, leased lines, and ISDN	No	Yes	Yes	No	Yes
Spain	Yes	Basic	No	Yes	Yes	Yes	No
Sweden	Yes	Basic and fax	No	No	Yes	Yes	Yes
United Kingdom	Yes	Basic	No	Yes	Yes	Yes	Yes

Source: Analysys Ltd., The Future of Universal Service in Telecommunications in Europe, Report 97-013 (Cambridge, England, 1997).

Table 1-3. *Monthly Charges for Residential Service in the EU, Canada, and United States, 1995*

U.S. dollars

Country	Monthly charge	Price per 3-minute local call	Average cost with 75 local calls per month
Australia	8.60	0.20	23.60
Austria	15.90	0.20	30.90
Belgium	18.80	0.20	33.80
Canada	8.10[a]	0	8.10
Denmark	17.80	0.20	32.80
Finland	7.10	0.10[a]	14.60
France	9.20	0.10	16.70
Germany	17.20	0.10	24.70
Greece	7.40	0[a]	7.40
Ireland	17.30[a]	0.20	32.30
Italy	8.60	0.20	23.60
Japan	18.60	0.10[a]	26.10
Luxembourg	7.60[a]	0.20	22.60
Netherlands	13.60	0.10	21.10
New Zealand	22.70	0[a]	22.70
Portugal	12.10	0.10	19.60
Spain	11.60	0.10	19.10
United Kingdom	13.00	0.20	28.00
United States	19.49	0	19.49

Source: International Telecommunication Union, *World Telecommunication Indicators* (Geneva, 1997), diskette. FCC, *Statistics of Communications Common Carriers 1997/1998* (1998), p. 320.
    a. 1994.

tial service over a terrestrial wire-based telephone network is likely to cost about $20 a month in urban areas and much more in rural areas. Therefore, countries such as Greece, Italy, and Spain have very large deficits in offering traditional local residential telephone service. In many of these countries, this deficit per line is surely greater than in the United States.

The European Commission has not directly ordered rate rebalancing, but its requirement that access deficits not be part of a Universal Service Fund in 2000 is putting pressure on individual governments to rebalance rates.[44] France began the process in 1997 with a 48 percent increase in local rates and a corresponding 47 percent reduction in long-distance rates. The

Netherlands allowed KPN Telecom to increase local rates by 27 percent in mid-1998 with corresponding reductions in calling charges.[45] However, Greece and Portugal have not yet begun rate rebalancing.[46] The United Kingdom, which began liberalization in 1984, provides an intermediate example. British Telecom was allowed to raise rates slowly through a price cap that was pegged to the annual change in the CPI plus 1.5 percent, an increase that BT took in every year through 1996 (except for 1986) when the constraint was removed. Even in those countries that have rebalanced, however, the monthly charge for a local line remains the same for urban and high-cost, rural areas. This remains an intractable issue that is not being addressed in most of Europe.

It seems that much of Europe has thus far avoided embracing new services in its universal service policies, perhaps because of lower Internet use in Europe than in North America. A survey of European national regulatory authorities and interest groups by Analysys Ltd. on behalf of the European Commission Directorate General XIII found that Europeans are not particularly supportive of broadening the definition of universal service to include new, innovative services.[47] Analysys reports that a broad consensus exists to separate the policies for diffusing new services from those of ensuring universality of ordinary telephone services, including directory assistance and access to emergency services. However, recent developments in France suggest that an expanded universal service obligation is a potentially important tool to protect the incumbent, France Telecom.

The French Telecommunications Act of 1996 defines universal service as "the provision to the public of a quality telephone service at an affordable price."[48] Besides the basic telephone service, the act defines universal service to include information services, directory services (printed and electronic), provision of pay phones in public places and the provision of free calls to emergency services as this is consistent with the EU directives.[49] Any operator with responsibility for universal service is required to provide service to any one who requests it. The act currently names France Telecom as the operator responsible for universal service, since the universal service obligation is *national* in scope although all telephone service providers are obliged to carry emergency calls free of charge.[50] Besides these obligations, all licensed network operators must offer a variety of other services, such as high-speed ISDN service, packet-switched data services, enhanced voice telephony, and leased lines.[51] The universal service obligations will be funded through interconnection charges (for as much as three years) and other levies on providers.

These French policies may have more to do with protecting France Telecom than with promoting universal service. In 1997 the deficit of France Telecom in providing local access (the "access deficit") was estimated as 4.5 billion French francs, or more than $700 million for a country that is one-fifth the size of the United States. By comparison, in the United Kingdom there is little or no access deficit according to the regulator, Oftel. Similarly, a recent study of Sweden, a long and sparsely populated country, concluded that the net cost of the universal service obligation for Telia—the incumbent telephone company—after accounting for various other "nonfinancial" benefits of incumbency was in the range of $5 million to $20 million a year, a negligible magnitude.[52]

Any universal service subsidies that remain must conform to the policies established in Directives 97/33 and 96/19.[53] These EU directives define the cost of universal service obligations as "the difference between the net costs of operating with and without universal service obligations," but it does not provide guidance on how such costs are to be measured or allocated across services or users. This cost must then be recovered through charges levied on public telecommunications providers in an objective, nondiscriminatory manner that does not penalize new entrants. However, it appears that in several countries the cost will be recovered from interconnection charges that must be paid by new entrants, thereby discouraging entry. Clearly, much thought must be given to structuring European universal service obligations in a manner compatible with a competitive environment.

Recent Studies of the Effectiveness of Universal Service Policies

Most analyses of universal service policies assume that the goal of such policies is to ensure that low-income and rural households subscribe to the basic telephone network. Such analyses may examine the effectiveness of universal service policies, their effect on economic efficiency, or both. We summarize only some of the more recent work here.

David L. Kaserman, John W. Mayo, and Joseph E. Flynn estimate a cross-sectional model of access rates (the carrier common line rates), residential rates, and residential telephone subscription in the mid-1980s.[54] Using only thirty-eight statewide observations, they find that an AT&T estimate of cross-subsidy per line has very little effect on U.S. residential rates and that residential telephone subscription has a very low price elasticity. Therefore, they conclude that the attempts to cross-subsidize local rates from long-distance revenues has little or no effect on universal service.

Milton L. Mueller and Jorge Reina Schement look in detail at telephone penetration in one low-income city, Camden, N.J.[55] They find that low penetration is not simply a function of low income. Renters and young households are less likely to have telephone service, in part because they are less creditworthy. Mueller and Schement find that a history of large long-distance bills is often responsible for the absence of a telephone because many customers fail to pay these bills and suffer a termination of service. However, the results of an interview survey they conducted suggest that cable television is generally more pervasive than telephones in part because some people receive cable TV illegally. Mueller and Schement conclude that usage costs are more important than network access costs in determining universal service.

In a sophisticated study of consumer expenditure patterns, Frank A. Wolak finds that expenditure elasticities for local telephone service are very low, but expenditure elasticities for long-distance service are high.[56] Unfortunately, his data, drawn from the Bureau of Labor Statistics' Consumer Expenditure Survey, do not permit him to match households with precise data on local and long-distance rates. Wolak therefore has only a rough approximation of the rates actually paid by his sample households. His analysis does not specifically examine the costs or benefits of universal service; rather, Wolak simply estimates the effect of raising local rates by 20 or 40 percent and reducing long-distance rates by 0, 20, or 40 percent. He concludes that raising local rates and reducing long-distance rates by the same proportion is welfare enhancing for all but a few households. Local expenditures rise very little for the average household with a 20 to 40 percent increase in local rates—presumably because second lines and vertical services decline—but long-distance expenditures rise substantially as long-distance rates are reduced by the same proportion.

More recently, Ross C. Eriksson, David L. Kaserman, and John A. Mayo examine the effect of universal service policies in 1984–93 by using pooled times-series, cross-section state data to estimate a recursive model of monthly local rates and subscriber demand.[57] They find exceedingly low elasticities of demand with respect to the monthly local rate, the installation rate, and long-distance rates within a state. Some of these estimates may be biased toward zero because of an errors-in-variables problem—

local rates vary across communities within each state, a problem that they cannot address because they use statewide data.[58] Nevertheless, Eriksson, Kaserman, and Mayo conclude that untargeted subsidies to local-exchange companies are much less efficient in promoting universal service than are the targeted programs (Lifeline and Link-Up). But even the targeted programs cost about $550 a year for each additional subscriber—certainly more than the cost of the service itself. Even these estimates are optimistic because they fail to take into account the negative effects on penetration from raising long-distance rates to fund these programs.

A study by Christopher Garbacz and Herbert G. Thompson uses 1990 Census of Population data to estimate the effect of subsidy programs on telephone penetration.[59] This study concludes that telephone penetration is more sensitive to the installation charge than to monthly rates, a reflection of the fact that many nonsubscribers are low-income households with unpaid previous bills and low creditworthiness. Paying the installation charge and, perhaps, back bills, serves as a more powerful disincentive to subscribing to the network than does the monthly rate in one of the authors' two models. While the targeted subsidy programs are successful in increasing telephone subscriptions, the elasticity of telephone penetration with respect to dollars spent on such programs is .003 to .008. Like Eriksson, Kaserman, and Mayo, they conclude that the likely effect of such subsidies, after accounting for the increase in long-distance rates to fund them, is minimal or even nonexistent.

Finally, Jerry Hausman looks at the efficiency of funding new universal service requirements in the United States—the new (new) universal service policy—from taxes on interstate telephone service.[60] He concludes that the cost of such subsidies is an additional $1.05 to $1.25 per $1.00 raised in subsidies, far above the cost of using general federal revenues for this purpose.

Conclusions

Most developed countries have some form of implicit subsidy program embedded in their telephone rate structure. Typically, these policies involve charging less than the long-run incremental cost for local residential connections and recovering the difference from usage charges for local, national, and international calls. These transfers are generally buried in the rate structure in a manner that makes them difficult for voters to detect.

In the United States, however, these implicit support payments from business and long-distance services are supplemented by direct subsidies paid from long-distance carrier charges to high-cost rural local telephone companies and to local companies offering discounted monthly rates and connection charges to qualifying (generally low-income) subscribers. These U.S. policies are now changing as a result of the 1996 Telecommunications Act. Federal universal service support is derived openly and directly from a tax (charge) levied on interstate carrier revenues. Furthermore, the United States is the most aggressive country in expanding the domain of services eligible for universal service subsidies. Universal service has been expanded to cover technologically advanced services provided to schools, libraries, and medical facilities.

Most studies of universal service policies conclude that they have minimal effect on telephone subscriptions. First, they are exceedingly broad and principally fund those who would subscribe anyway (such as readers of this book). Second, these policies do not address the real causes of nonsubscription—installation fees and excessive past bills for long-distance calling. Finally, the taxes levied to pay for these subsidies are on calling—local and long-distance—taxes that feed back on the nonpayment problem. Perhaps more important is that there are substantial adverse effects on economic welfare owing to how these taxes are levied. We delve into this problem in the following chapters when we estimate the cost of current universal service policies and the likely costs of extending such programs to new telecommunications services in the United States.

2 | *Telephone Service versus Other Household Services*

Why is telephone service any different from scores of other household services, such as household plumbing, electricity, refrigeration of household food stocks, or even the services of a television set? Among all of these services, telephone service stands out as the only service (or durable product) for which there is a public policy designed to provide vast numbers of people access to it at prices below the costs of serving them. This subsidy on access is invariably paid for by raising the prices of access for other subscribers above cost (residential subscribers in densely populated areas and businesses in most areas) and by raising the price of using the service—calling—above its cost. Such a policy is defended as essential to promote universal service, but why are similar policies not pursued for other essential household services?[1]

The Case for Universal Service: Externalities

It is easy to argue that the telephone provides social connectivity and enables individuals to readily gain access to needed services—ambulance, fire, police, or other emergency services. There are also economic reasons—the presence of externalities—that have been advanced to explain why the price of connecting to the network should be held below its costs. These externalities include network externalities, call externalities, and social externalities.

Positive externalities are generated by the action of one individual that benefits others without a corresponding payment, or revenue flow, to the individual generating them. The traditional example is the beekeeper who sets up next to an orchard. The bees, while collecting pollen, improve the productivity of the orchard. The orchard owner, by planting more trees, increases the flow of honey. However, without a financial flow, either from orchard owner to beekeeper or vice versa, no incentive exists for either one to invest sufficiently for both operations, since neither shares in the external benefits he generates for the other. Given these externalities, some form of compensation or social intervention can increase social welfare.

Two points are important. First, as an empirical analysis by Steven Cheung concludes, it is obvious to the beekeeper and the orchard owner that their neighborliness confers benefits.[2] In fact, Cheung finds that a market often does arise to internalize these benefits, either through direct payments or through vertical integration in which the positive benefits of the relationship are recognized. Indeed, Ronald Coase recognized forty years ago that property rights will evolve in a fashion that ensures an efficient outcome when such externalities exist.[3]

Second, few real life examples of positive externalities are cited in the literature of applied economics. Much more prevalent in this literature are negative externalities, such as environmental pollution. A factory emitting toxic waste may damage distant citizens who cannot determine the source of their discomfort or avoid these effects even if they can identify the sources. In this case, a natural market mechanism (or internalization) is unlikely to evolve over time.[4]

NETWORK EXTERNALITIES.   Since the value of a network rises with the number of members, an additional connection to the system increases the benefit of the network to all users. Because an individual's decision to acquire service is based solely on his or her calculation of its benefits and costs, the benefits to others of this decision to join the network are not taken into account. Hence, it is argued that a suboptimal number of individuals may join the network.[5]

The network externality in telephone networks may be characterized fairly simply. What I am willing to pay to join a network is a function of how many others I can call (and who can call me). The standard economic analysis of this externality concludes that the *n*th person to join a network should pay a price below her costs to induce her to subscribe. She does not, in evaluating the costs and benefits of a telephone, consider the benefits she provides to others. As a result, the externalities are analogous to the case of pollution because of the impossibility of identifying the beneficiaries, who otherwise might be induced to compensate her directly. The alternative is to provide a general societal subsidy for network subscriptions even though those who pay for the subsidy may not be the direct beneficiaries from expanded network subscriptions.[6]

The theory underlying such a subsidy is formally correct; however, it is apparent that neither all residential consumers nor all rural consumers need to be subsidized because of such a network externality. It is necessary to subsidize only those individuals whose private benefits do not exceed the costs of serving them, but who generate sufficient external benefits to make up the difference. Given that telephone bills account for a small share of total household expenditures, it is only some poor households—and probably not all such households—who may require such a subsidy in order to subscribe to telephone service.

Moreover, the network externality argument has little if any relevance for telephony in developed economies today for several reasons. If my telephone in Manhattan reaches 2 million people, another connection will probably have little value to me. Of course, if that connection is my mother, then the connection is of real value to me, and, as in the beekeeper and orchard owner example, I can subsidize her telephone directly! Otherwise, there is no reason why I—in Manhattan—should subsidize someone in Kalamazoo.[7]

CALL EXTERNALITIES.   Another source of externalities has been identified by Lester Taylor.[8] His estimates of telecommunications demand functions show that a call generates other calls. When one person calls another, the second calls a third person, thereby generating an externality to this third person. But this externality provides no reason to subsidize access by taxing calling. In fact, it suggests that the recipient should be billed for part of the cost of the call, not that her monthly line should be subsidized.

SOCIAL EXTERNALITIES.   The social externality argument may be the most powerful. Individuals need telephones to be connected to society or to call for help in case of a police, fire, or medical emergency. In such an emergency, a person without a telephone would be willing to pay a very high price to have a telephone. A telephone for every household could be a social goal to which we all subscribe and to which we all contribute. It is important to consider, however, that for most people who do not have a telephone or who have had service disconnected, the long-distance bill, that is, the price of calling is the most important barrier to universality.

One can use any or all of these arguments to justify the pricing of telephone access below its incremental cost—at least for some households. But there are Coasian alternatives.[9] For instance, a business that depends on connecting to retail customers would want to maximize residential penetration and hence might be willing to pay part of the costs of an individual's access. This may explain part of the large price differential between business and residential access. However, many businesses do not rely on households for their sales, and these companies would want maximum penetration among other businesses. Yet the price to all business users, at least those in urban areas, is generally above the long-run incremental cost of the service,[10] suggesting that the externality argument is not correctly applied in reality.

Finally, the externality argument would suggest subsidizing only those users (residential and business) who would not otherwise subscribe at a price equal to incremental cost, but in most countries (including the United States) rates are set for broad groups of subscribers, providing large classes of users—such as rural residents, rich and poor—with below-cost access, but not targeting such support on individuals whose willingness or ability to subscribe is in doubt. These pricing patterns cannot be justified by the externality argument.

Why should telephony be accorded a higher social priority than other household services or even household durables? If we are to ensure that everyone has telephone service, are there not also valid social-externality arguments for a universal service policy for radio, television, or even indoor plumbing? The market is generally thought to provide these important services reasonably well. It may come as a surprise that many of these services are even more widespread than is telephone service.

Surprisingly, expenditures on telephone service are not a very large share of even the lowest-income households' budgets in the high-income countries. These households typically spend much more on other necessities, such as food, clothing, and shelter. Perhaps more important, many spend as much or more on tobacco, alcohol, or personal-care products as they do on the telephone, suggesting that they can readily afford to pay for telephone service. In the remainder of this chapter, we examine the degree to which households obtain essential durables and services without the aid of a "universal service" policy and the pattern of household expenditures on a variety of necessities and otherwise mundane items.

The Need for Universal Service Policies in Developed Countries

One might make a case for intervention in telephone pricing decisions to ensure universal access to telephone service if there were large social gains from such a policy. These gains would emerge in the form of the increase in households connecting to the network. But in most developed countries, virtually everyone is already connected to the network. The International Telecommunication Union—an intergovernmental association for the telephone sector—publishes detailed statistics on telephone service for more than 200 countries. Its principal measure of telephone penetration, shown in table 2-1, is the number of main (primary) lines per 100 inhabitants. Unfortunately this measure includes business and residential lines, but it is still useful.[11] In most developed countries, more than 70 percent of lines are residential lines; hence, given about 2.5 persons per household in developed countries, any number above fifty-one in table 2-1 suggests a residential penetration of 90 percent and perhaps more.

The seventy-four countries in table 2-1 are aggregated into four income classes based on annual average per capita income: low income (less than U.S. $750), lower middle income (between $750 and $2,500), upper middle income (between $2,500 and $7,500) and high income (above $7,500). Note that penetration rates clearly rise with income. In 1995 the average penetration rate in low-income countries was fewer than two phones per 100 inhabitants; in lower-middle-income countries the penetration rate was ten; in upper-middle-income countries, twenty-six; and in high-income countries, fifty to sixty. By contrast, as recently as 1980, the penetration rate was only thirty phones per 100 inhabitants in high-income countries, ten in upper-middle-income countries, three in lower-middle-income countries, and fewer than one in low-income countries.

Clearly, penetration has increased dramatically in fifteen years, even in high-income countries. In 1995 only ten of the twenty-two high-income countries shown in the table had fewer than fifty lines per 100 households, a level of telephone penetration that reflects virtual universality of residential service. Thus these developed countries have largely achieved the goals

Table 2-1. *Telephone Penetration across Countries, 1980 and 1995*

Main telephone lines per 100 population

Low income	1980	1995	Lower middle income	1980	1995	Upper middle income	1980	1995	High income	1980	1995
Viet Nam	...	1.05	Philippines	0.87	2.09	Czech Republic	11.46	23.65	Israel	22.16	41.77
Tanzania	0.21	0.30	Angola	0.51	0.56	Hungary	5.76	18.53	Bahamas	14.80	...
Uganda	0.15	0.23	Ecuador	2.85	6.52	Brazil	3.71	7.48	Ireland	14.20	36.53
Egypt	...	4.63	El Salvador	1.52	5.28	Trinidad and Tobago	3.99	16.04	Spain	19.34	38.50
Pakistan	0.36	1.62	Cameroon	...	0.45	Russia	7.00	16.99	New Zealand	36.15	47.85
India	0.31	1.29	Dominican Republic	1.90	7.28	Argentina	6.68	15.99	Hong Kong	25.38	53.25
Nigeria	...	0.36	Colombia	4.06	9.98	S. Korea	7.09	41.47	Singapore	22.22	47.85
China	0.22	3.35	Congo	0.51	0.81	Portugal	10.67	36.15	U.K.	32.24	50.25
Kenya	0.45	0.90	Peru	1.75	4.71	S. Arabia	3.33	9.62	Australia	32.27	50.97
Ghana	0.35	0.35	Thailand	0.78	5.86	Barbados	17.98	34.53	Germany	33.19	49.35
Nicaragua	1.10	2.34	Poland	5.46	14.84	Taiwan	13.05	43.07	Netherlands	34.57	52.52
Zambia	0.57	0.82	Jamaica	2.47	11.56	Greece	23.55	49.32	Italy	23.07	43.35
Haiti	...	0.84	Turkey	2.57	21.16	Kuwait	11.42	22.61	Belgium	24.80	45.75
Guyana	...	5.30	Iran	2.33	7.57				Canada	40.58	58.97
Indonesia	0.25	1.69	Panama	6.50	11.42				Austria	29.02	46.55
Zimbabwe	1.34	1.40	Chile	3.26	13.20				France	29.51	55.80
Honduras	0.81	2.87	Algeria	1.66	4.21				Japan	34.18	48.80
			Bulgaria	10.25	30.57				Norway	29.30	55.85
			Malaysia	2.87	16.56				Denmark	43.43	61.26
			Venezuela	5.30	11.09				Sweden	58.00	68.11
			Uruguay	7.55	19.56				Finland	36.38	55.01
									Bermuda	41.43	83.47
									Switzerland	44.46	61.34
Average	0.5	1.6	Average	3.0	10	Average	9.7	26	Average	30.2	50.0

Source: International Telecommunication Union (ITU), *World Telecommunication Indicators* (Geneva, 1997), diskette.

of universal service. In later chapters, we investigate whether below-cost monthly connection rates are required to maintain this universality of telephone subscription.

In upper-middle-income countries, only South Korea, Taiwan, and Greece approach universal service. For every other country in the world, universal voice telephone service is still merely a goal. In a subsequent chapter, we show that the low levels of telephone penetration for low-income countries reflect not only the low purchasing power of households in these countries but the very high connection and calling charges established by their national telephone carriers.[12] However, the differences in penetration evidenced in table 2-1 are somewhat overstated because of the differences in the queues—or waiting lists—of households and businesses for telephone service. These waiting lists, enumerated in table 2-2, reflect those individuals who declare their willingness to have a telephone at the existing prices but have not been connected to the network by their inefficient national telephone companies. These waiting lists could well be an underestimate of excess demand. In low-income countries waiting lists average 47 percent of the existing lines; in lower-middle-income countries, 34 percent; in upper-middle-income countries, 15 percent; and in the most developed countries, essentially zero.

In short, for ordinary voice-grade telephone service there is simply no universal service problem in the world's richest countries. This state of affairs is not because of these countries' pricing policies, as figures 2-1 and 2-2 demonstrate. There is virtually no relationship between monthly residential rates or the residential connection charge and the number of telephones per capita in the richest countries—the OECD countries for which there are data. By contrast, even in OECD countries, a mild positive correlation shows up between real GDP per capita and telephone lines per capita (figure 2-3). The wealthiest of the wealthy countries undoubtedly have more business and residential lines per person, but those that hold down the residential rate for leasing a line, perhaps through universal service policies, do not appear to enjoy higher telephone penetration rates.[13]

The departures from universal service are substantial, however, in lower-income countries, and the problem is exacerbated by their telephone companies' inability to deliver the service to those who desire it at current prices and income levels. In many of these countries, very high installation charges exclude a large share of the population from telephone service. Therefore, even to approach universal service in these low-income countries requires attention to the supply side and the demand side of the market.

Table 2-2. *Waiting Lists for Telephone Service, 1995*
Percent of lines

Low income		Lower middle income		Upper middle income		High income	
Viet Nam	33	Philippines	60	Czech Republic	26	Israel	0
Tanzania	161	Angola	...	Hungary	37	Bahamas	14
Uganda	9	Ecuador	9	Brazil	4	Ireland	0
Zaire	17	El Salvador	70	Trinidad and	4	Spain	0
Pakistan	14	Cameroon	50	Tobago		N. Zealand	0
India	18	Dominican	2	Russia	43	Hong Kong	0
Nigeria	48	Republic		Argentina	9	Singapore	0
China	4	Colombia	20	S. Korea	0	U.K.	0
Kenya	29	Congo	4	Portugal	0	Australia	0
Ghana	21	Peru	25	S. Arabia	63	Germany	0
Nicaragua	33	Thailand	46	Barbados	3	Netherlands	0
Zambia	93	Poland	41	Taiwan	0	Italy	0
Haiti	38	Jamaica	58	Greece	4	Belgium	0
Guyana	68	Turkey	5	Kuwait	1	Canada	0
Indonesia	4	Iran	23			Austria	0
Zimbabwe	70	Panama	6			France	0
Honduras	143	Chile	6			Japan	0
Egypt	48	Algeria	55			Norway	0
		Bulgaria	22			Sweden	0
		Malaysia	4			Finland	0
		Venezuela	37			Bermuda	0
		Uruguay	15			Denmark	0
						Switzerland	0
Average	47	Average	34	Average	15	Average	1

Source: ITU, *World Telecommunication Indicators*, 1997, diskette.

The Universality of Other Household Goods and Services

One might argue persuasively for a set of policies (subsidies) to induce households to connect to the telephone network if large numbers of these households would not subscribe at unsubsidized, cost-based rates and if the additional subscribers conferred substantial external benefits on others. However, we show that even with cost-based telephone rates, very few households in developed countries would choose not to subscribe. Given that telephone service accounts for a very small share of even lower-income

Figure 2-1. *Monthly Rates versus Telephone Lines, OECD*

Monthly residential rate (U.S. dollars)

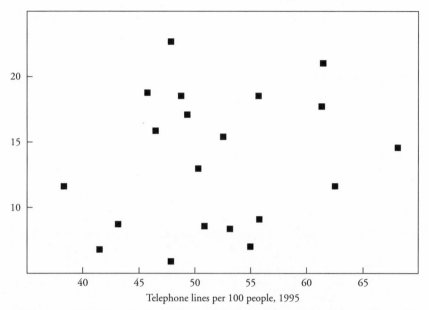

Telephone lines per 100 people, 1995

Source: International Telecommunication Union (ITU), *World Telecommunication Indicators* (Geneva, 1997), diskette.

households' budgets in wealthy countries, there is little need to worry that many of these households would shun the benefits of modern telephony.

Direct statistical evidence on the price-insensitivity of the household demand for telephone service is presented in chapter 5. However, for the present, we show that in most OECD countries, virtually universal access to a wide array of household durables and services is achieved without the inducement of universal service subsidies. In some cases more households choose voluntarily to avail themselves of these unsubsidized durables or services than to connect to subsidized telephone service. This is not to suggest that all such durables or services are subject to the same consumption externalities as is telephone service but merely to demonstrate that universality of modern durable goods and services is regularly achieved in high-income countries without government intervention.

Though we would like to provide information across developed countries for a uniform set of durables or services, the available data do not

Figure 2-2. *Residential Connection Charge versus Telephone Lines, OECD*

Connection charge (U.S. dollars)

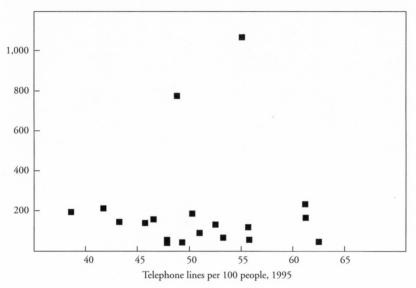

Telephone lines per 100 people, 1995

Source: ITU, *World Telecommunication Indicators.*

permit such a uniform approach. Therefore, we provide information on a somewhat different set of durables or services for the United States, Canada, Japan, and various European countries.

The United States

Statistics on the share of households with various modern durables or services have been collected by the U.S. Census Bureau for decades. A few of the more important recent data are summarized in table 2-3. In addition, the Department of Energy conducts a periodic survey of U.S. households to determine energy usage and a variety of household characteristics, including the ownership of appliances. The most recent data are available for 1993 and are arrayed by income category in table 2-4. Note that more U.S. homes have complete plumbing, radio and television sets, refrigerators, ovens, and water heaters than telephones, a relationship that has persisted for decades for many of these durables. This is especially true for low-income households. Apparently, even though telephone service is of-

Figure 2-3. *Real GDP versus Telephone Lines, OECD*

Real GDP per capita (1996 U.S. dollars)

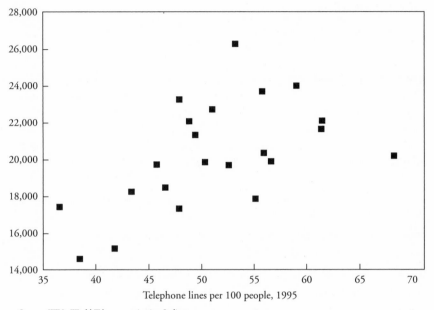

Telephone lines per 100 people, 1995

Source: ITU, *World Telecommunication Indicators.*

Table 2-3. *The Diffusion of Various Consumer Durables and Services in the United States, 1970–94*

Percent of households

Item	1970	1980	1990	1994
Radio	98.6	99.0	99.0	99.0
Television set	95.3	97.9	98.2	98.3
Cable television service	6.7	19.9	56.4	62.4
Telephone service	87.0	93.0	93.3	93.9
Complete plumbing	93.1	97.3	98.9	97.7[a]

Source: Bureau of the Census, *Statistical Abstract of the United States, 1995* (Government Printing Office, 1995), tables 897, 1224.

a. 1995 data (*Statistical Abstract of the United States, 1997,* table 1196).

Table 2-4. *U.S. Ownership of Selected Durables and Telephone Service, by Income, 1993*

Percent of households

Annual income (U.S. $)	Clothes washer	Clothes dryer	Oven	Refrigerator	Television set	Water heater	Telephone
Less than 5,000	47.9	33.8	96.8	99.5	95.9	97.6	72.9
5,000–9,999	55.6	43.4	95.3	99.3	97.9	98.3	85.7
10,000–14,999	63.6	52.7	95.6	100	97.7	98.3	91.3
15,000–24,999	74.2	68.1	97.6	99.8	98.8	99.1	94.9
25,000–34,999	83.8	80.7	98.3	99.8	99.3	99.1	98.0
35,000–49,999	85.1	82.3	98.7	100	99.1	99.1	98.9
50,000 or more	92	89.2	98.6	100	99.6	99.1	99.5
All	77.1	71.2	97.6	99.8	98.8	98.9	94.2

Sources: Department of Energy, Energy Information Administration, *Household Characteristics, 1993*; and telephone data from Federal Communications Commission (FCC), "Monitoring Report: June 1999," table 6.5.

fered at flat monthly rates that are often below the long-run incremental cost of the line, many low-income households view a refrigerator, oven, or TV set as a more pressing need than telephone access.

The explanation for the diffusion of plumbing service in the United States, even for low-income renters, may be the enforcement of housing codes that require such facilities, but this is surely not the explanation for radios and television sets. Furthermore, although fewer households in every income category have washing machines and dryers than telephones, these facilities may well be available in apartment buildings but not in the household's living quarters. Obviously, telephone services can also be provided in this manner through pay telephones.

Canada

Canadian households exhibit much the same pattern of consumer-durable ownership as do U.S. households. Recent data on durables ownership are shown in table 2-5. As in the United States, lower-income households in Canada are more likely to have a color television set and a refrigerator than a telephone. The penetration of clothes washers and dryers is almost as high as telephone penetration even though there is surely no universal service policy for either.

Table 2-5. *Canadian Ownership of Selected Durables and Services,
by Income, 1996*
Percent of households

Annual income (Canadian $)	Clothes washer	Clothes dryer	Refrigerator	Color television set	Cable TV	Telephone
Less than 15,000	75.7	51.5	98.1	96.6	65.6	90.1
15,000–19,999	93.2	78.2	100	97.9	81.5	95.7
20,000–24,999	95.5	86.5	100	98.5	81.4	97.2
25,000–34,999	93.0	84.9	100	99.5	82.8	98.4
35,000–44,999	93.1	86.1	100	99.0	88.3	100
45,000–54,999	94.9	94.2	100	100	91.9	100
55,000–69,999	100	96.5	99.3	100	91.1	100
70,000 or more	99.4	98.8	100	98.7	94.7	99.3

Source: Statistics Canada.

Europe

Given their high levels of per capita income, it is not surprising that most western European countries exhibit penetration rates for household durables that approach those of the United States and Canada. The data in table 2-6 are for a sample of European countries covering a fairly wide range of GDP per capita. Unfortunately, the aggregate data are available only through 1988, and those by income quartile are only available through 1984. Given the growth in GDP since 1988, more recent data would certainly show a growth in the penetration of most durables. For our purposes, it is important to note that even by 1988 many of these durable-goods penetration rates were close to the penetration rates for telephone service. The exception is Ireland, whose households appear to prefer washing machines and color television sets to telephone service. In every country shown in table 2-6, an inside bathroom is more prevalent than a telephone.

More detailed data are available by income class for a few countries. Recent data for France, displayed in table 2-7, show that the poorest French households are still more likely to have a television set, a refrigerator, and indoor plumbing than a telephone.

The United Kingdom also has quite recent detailed data—both for durables ownership and household expenditures—arrayed by household

Table 2-6. *Household Penetration Rates for Selected Durables in Selected European Countries, 1988*
Percent of households

Country	Color television	Washing machine	Deep freezer	Inside bathroom	Telephone
Denmark	86.4	66.0	89.0	97.0	94.0
Greece	51.4	69.8	3.2	84.6	74.8
France	83.8	85.6	44.1	93.5	92.7
Ireland	81.8	77.1	n.a.	93.9	54.3
Luxembourg	90.2	94.7	71.9	99.4	97.8
Netherlands	88.7	89.6	39.6	n.a.	95.7

Source: Eurostat, 1992 Family Budget.
n.a. = Not available.

income. Table 2-8 shows the distribution of washing machines, VCRs, and telephones in the United Kingdom. Given its lower GDP per capita, the United Kingdom exhibits somewhat lower penetration of household durables than do higher-income countries, such as France, Luxembourg, or Canada, but washing machines enjoy almost as high household penetration as the telephone despite the absence of universal service subsidies for the former.

Table 2-7. *French Ownership of Selected Durables, by Income, 1995*
Percent of households

Annual income (francs)	Television set	Refrigerator	Washing machine	Inside bathroom	Telephone
Less than 88,000	90.4	96.5	77.8	92.3	87.8
88,000–115,000	95.9	97.7	87.2	95.8	95.1
115,000–140,000	97.0	98.7	88.9	97.1	97.2
140,000–157,000	95.7	99.3	90.1	97.3	98.1
157,000–189,000	96.5	99.2	90.8	99.0	97.3
209,000–239,000	94.9	98.8	91.6	99.7	99.0
239,000 or more	94.6	98.6	92.5	99.5	99.1
Average	95.0	98.4	88.5	97.3	96.3

Source: National Institute of Statistics and Economic Studies (INSEE), *La Consommation des Menages en 1995* (Paris, 1995).

Table 2-8. *Household Penetration Rates of Telephones, Washing Machines, and VCRs in the United Kingdom, 1995–96*
Percent of households

Income decile	Telephone	Washing machine	VCR
Lowest	76.5	72.2	46.2
Second	85.6	81.3	59.6
Third	88.2	86.5	63.4
Fourth	90.1	88.4	75.4
Fifth	92.6	93.4	83.2
Sixth	95.3	95.0	89.5
Seventh	98.1	96.9	91.6
Eighth	98.7	98.7	94.6
Ninth	99.4	97.6	93.2
Highest	99.9	99.4	95.1
Average	92.4	90.9	79.2

Source: United Kingdom Office for National Statistics, *1995–96 Family Expenditure Survey.*

Household Expenditures: How Burdensome Is the Monthly Telephone Bill?

As we have shown, many household durables and services are virtually universal in high-income countries without the assistance of any overt government universal service policy. What about other household expenditures in relation to the monthly telephone bill? A comparison of outlays for telephone service with those for other household necessities or even nonnecessities can shed some light. If telephone bills are not a large share of the outlays by even the less affluent households, the case for subsidizing local telephone connections is surely weakened.

The United States

Consumer expenditure patterns reveal a good deal about household preferences. In the next chapter, we analyze household spending patterns for telephone services in several countries. For now, we compare the average spending on simply connecting to the telephone network, that is, on local service, and on total telephone service with other household expenditures. These data, arrayed by household income, are shown in table 2-9. Note that local telephone expenditures do not rise much with

Table 2-9. *Average Annual Household Expenditures in the United States, by Income, 1995*

U.S. dollars (percent of household expenditures)

Annual income (percent of households)	Food	Shelter	Entertainment	Tobacco	Personal care products	Alcohol	Local telephone service	Total telephone expenditure
Less than 5,000 (5.6)	2,519 (17.1)	3,275 (22.2)	720 (4.9)	213 (1.4)	188 (1.3)	102 (0.7)	274[a] (1.9)	483 (3.3)
5,000–9,999 (11.7)	2,374 (16.9)	3,020 (21.3)	664 (4.7)	197 (1.4)	182 (1.3)	102 (0.7)	267[b] (1.9)	490 (3.5)
10,000–14,999 (10.5)	3,073 (16.2)	3,774 (20.0)	890 (4.7)	199 (1.1)	274 (1.4)	194 (1.0)	268 (1.4)	542 (2.9)
15,000–19,999 (9.3)	3,883 (17.2)	4,142 (18.3)	903 (4.0)	276 (1.2)	299 (1.3)	180 (0.8)	293 (1.3)	623 (2.8)
20,000–29,999 (15.2)	4,065 (15.2)	4,557 (17.1)	1,217 (4.3)	309 (1.2)	366 (1.4)	219 (0.8)	289 (1.1)	669 (2.5)
30,000–39,999 (12.8)	4,710 (14.1)	5,868 (17.6)	1,764 (5.3)	324 (1.0)	450 (1.4)	243 (0.7)	293 (0.9)	758 (2.3)
40,000–49,999 (9.8)	5,499 (14.2)	6,318 (16.4)	1,924 (5.0)	275 (0.7)	542 (1.4)	378 (1.0)	295 (0.8)	761 (2.0)
50,000–69,999 (12.4)	6,229 (12.8)	7,793 (16.0)	2,509 (5.1)	339 (0.7)	599 (1.2)	459 (0.9)	313 (0.6)	876 (1.8)
70,000 or more (12.7)	8,030 (11.6)	12,312 (17.8)	3,781 (5.4)	258 (0.4)	769 (1.1)	677 (1.0)	324 (0.5)	1,012 (1.5)

Sources: Bureau of Labor Statistics, *Consumer Expenditure Survey* (Department of Labor, 1995); and local telephone and associates' service data provided by PNR, *Bill Harvesting Survey II* (Jenkintown, Pa., 1995).

a. Data for income level $0–$7,499.

b. Data for income level $7,500–$9,999.

household income because few households have more than one line or
purchase many vertical services, such as call waiting. Most households
spend less money on local telephone service than on personal care products, such as deodorant and shampoo. At every income level, households
spend more income on entertainment—and those who smoke (about 25
percent of the adult population) spend much more on cigarettes—than
they do on local telephone service. Unless there are large externalities in
attracting marginal telephone subscribers, there would appear to be little
reason to provide below-cost local-telephone connections for the few
lower-income households that might choose not to have telephone service
but can afford larger expenditures on toiletries and tobacco.

At the current price of flat-rate local service in the United States, about
$20 a month, the average household spends less than 0.9 percent of its
income on a local telephone line. Even the lowest-income households
shown in table 2-9 spend less than 3.3 percent of their annual budgets on
telephone service, far less than they spend on entertainment and about
what they spend on tobacco, alcohol, and personal care products combined.[14] Of their total telephone expenditures, about half—or 1.9 percent
of total spending—is spent on local service. The regressivity of any attempt
to provide local telephone service at below-cost rates may be seen in the
high-income households' spending on such service. By keeping the price
of local service low to all residences, regulators allow high-income consumers to connect to the network by spending only 0.5 percent or less of their
budgets on local telephone service even though these households are much
more likely to have second lines or additional local services.[15]

Canada

The distribution of Canadian household expenditures across income
classes is similar to that of the United States. Canadians tend to allocate a
smaller share of their household expenditures to shelter and slightly more
to tobacco products. Otherwise their expenditures for the selected expenditure categories shown in table 2-10 are similar to those for U.S. households (table 2-9). In every income class, the average Canadian household
spends far more on tobacco or products for personal care than on local
telephone service because local rates are very low in Canada. Indeed, the
average household in every income class spends more on tobacco than on
total telephone service.[16]

Table 2-10. *Average Annual Household Expenditures in Canada, by Income, 1992*
U.S. Dollars (percent of household expenditures)

Annual income (percent of households)	Food	Shelter	Entertainment	Tobacco	Personal care products	Local telephone (basic charge)	Total telephone
Less than 5,000 (0.9)	2,268 (17.0)	2,794 (21.0)	516 (3.9)	324 (2.4)	235 (1.8)	141 (1.0)	284 (2.1)
5,000–9,999 (8.2)	1,917 (20.1)	2,697 (28.2)	321 (3.4)	345 (3.6)	238 (2.5)	174 (1.5)	281 (2.9)
10,000–14,999 (10.5)	2,682 (18.8)	3,149 (22.1)	612 (4.3)	475 (3.3)	369 (2.6)	179 (1.0)	370 (2.6)
15,000–19,999 (9.6)	3,223 (16.9)	3,625 (19.0)	749 (3.9)	558 (2.9)	457 (2.4)	185 (0.8)	424 (2.2)
20,000–29,999 (18.0)	3,923 (14.8)	4,136 (15.6)	1,095 (4.1)	689 (2.6)	585 (2.2)	189 (0.6)	468 (1.8)
30,000–39,999 (16.1)	4,769 (13.5)	5,004 (14.1)	1,528 (4.3)	758 (2.1)	693 (2.0)	198 (0.5)	512 (1.4)
40,000–49,999 (12.4)	5,390 (12.2)	5,639 (12.8)	1,962 (4.4)	810 (1.8)	827 (1.9)	203 (0.4)	536 (1.2)
50,000–69,999 (14.2)	6,215 (11.2)	6,582 (11.9)	2,565 (4.6)	767 (1.4)	982 (1.8)	212 (0.3)	591 (1.1)
70,000 or more (9.9)	7,905 (9.5)	8,869 (10.7)	3,582 (4.3)	766 (0.9)	1,247 (1.5)	231 (0.2)	703 (0.8)

Source: Statistics Canada, *Family Expenditure in Canada 1992.*

Table 2-11. *Average Annual Household Expenditures in France, by Income, 1995*

Francs

Annual income	Alcohol	Tobacco	Food away from home	Toilet articles	Electricity	Telephone
Less than 88,000	1,491	2,001	3,243	1,371	2,593	2,022
88,000–115,000	2,024	1,879	3,473	1,586	2,985	2,252
115,000–140,000	2,375	1,717	4,176	1,764	3,094	2,250
140,000–157,000	2,583	1,564	5,066	1,992	3,189	2,456
157,000–189,000	2,923	1,815	7,121	2,292	3,103	2,706
189,000–239,000	3,231	1,665	7,739	2,413	3,357	2,892
239,000 or more	4,059	1,482	12,411	2,852	3,510	3,925
Average	2,693	1,726	6,273	2,052	3,126	2,664

Source: INSEE, *Le Budget des Menages en 1995* (Paris, 1995).

Europe

European family expenditure patterns are similar to the United States and Canadian data. For instance, French expenditures on alcohol, tobacco, or toiletry articles (personal care) are almost as large as spending on telephone service among lower-income households (table 2-11). Even the lowest-income families spend more on food away from home than on telephone service, and about as much on tobacco products. Higher-income families spend more on alcohol than on telephone service.

In all income classes, the average Briton spends more income on alcohol or tobacco than on telephone service, and most spend far more on personal goods and services than on telephone service (table 2-12).

Our final example from a European country comes from Hungary, a country with a decidedly lower average income per capita than the EU countries analyzed thus far. Even in Hungary, households spend more on tobacco, alcohol, or personal care items than on telephone service (table 2-13). Part of the reason, however, is that telephone penetration in Hungary is only about one-third of that in EU countries (table 2-6). If we divide the reported expenditures on telephone service by one-third, we may obtain an approximate measure of the average expenditure per household *with a telephone*. Even with this adjustment, the average household with a telephone spends more income on alcohol and tobacco combined than on telephone service.

Table 2-12. *Average Weekly Household Expenditures in the United Kingdom, by Income Decile, 1994–95*

Pounds

Decile	Alcohol	Tobacco	Personal goods and services	Video entertainment	Electricity	Telephone
Lowest	3.11	3.78	2.18	1.70	4.91	2.52
Second	3.49	4.14	4.14	2.34	5.69	3.34
Third	5.48	5.37	5.33	2.41	5.98	3.87
Fourth	7.75	5.80	7.49	2.54	6.14	4.44
Fifth	11.32	5.77	10.23	2.50	6.78	4.77
Sixth	13.22	6.87	10.59	2.87	6.32	4.85
Seventh	15.45	5.87	13.28	2.95	7.03	5.30
Eighth	16.84	6.46	14.01	3.08	6.98	5.64
Ninth	20.05	5.92	17.23	2.97	7.79	6.39
Highest	26.54	6.10	22.60	2.95	8.79	7.57
Average	12.32	5.61	10.78	2.63	6.64	4.87

Source: United Kingdom Office for National Statistics, *1995–96 Family Expenditure Survey, 1994–95.*

Table 2-13. *Average Annual Household Expenditures in Hungary, by Income Decile, 1993*

Forint

Decile	Personal care	Alcohol	Tobacco	Electricity	Television license	Telephone
Lowest	1,511	1,155	3,193	2,313	762	428
Second	1,822	1,869	3,441	2,868	1,044	668
Third	1,969	1,971	2,929	3,046	1,108	765
Fourth	2,128	2,373	2,951	3,353	1,223	922
Fifth	1,989	2,026	2,993	3,407	1,227	1,037
Sixth	2,188	2,688	2,569	3,514	1,330	1,015
Seventh	2,215	2,877	3,124	3,919	1,304	1,646
Eighth	2,888	3,098	2,888	4,210	1,477	2,067
Ninth	3,220	3,784	3,383	4,384	1,444	2,028
Highest	4,386	5,336	3,847	5,132	1,702	3,509
Average	2,431	2,717	3,132	3,615	1,266	1,408

Source: Hungarian Central Statistical Office, *1993 Hungarian Household Budget Survey.*

Table 2-14. *Average Monthly Household Expenditures in Japan, by Income, 1994*
Yen

Annual income (10,000 Y)	Total expenditure	Toilet articles	Alcohol	Tobacco	Fuel, light, and water	Telephone
Less than 200	172,961	1,855	2,548	1,298	14,417	4,313
400–450	254,296	2,713	3,635	1,361	16,269	4,798
600–650	305,170	3,406	4,294	1,195	17,958	5,313
800–900	372,893	3,983	4,817	1,217	20,077	5,868
1,000–1,250	444,009	4,785	5,010	1,068	21,796	6,513
2,000 or more	601,816	6,196	5,481	1,221	28,281	8,261
Average	344,066	3,722	4,428	1,232	19,107	5,667

Source: Government of Japan, Statistics Bureau, Management and Coordination Agency, *1994 National Japanese Survey of Income and Expenditure.*

Japan

Japanese households spend a far smaller share of their income than do the citizens of most other developed countries. Expenditures on such items as alcohol, tobacco, or toilet articles are small compared with those by Western European and North American households (table 2-14), yet spending on tobacco plus alcohol is about the same as on telephone service. Household expenditures on telephone service in Japan are similar to those in the United States and Canada at lower income levels (between 2 and 3 percent of household expenditures), but upper-income Japanese households spend decidedly less on telephone service than their North American counterparts. This suggests that the price elasticity of demand for long-distance calls in Japan must be quite high at the extremely high Japanese long-distance rates.

Conclusion

Much of the information in this chapter on the diffusion of household durables or consumer expenditure patterns is hardly the source of profound new insights about consumer behavior. We show it simply to cast some light on the ubiquity and affordability of telephone service. Many other services, including the services of what we now consider common household durables, are available universally to all households in developed countries without a complex policy of pricing distortions to induce their purchase. More important, telephone service is such a small part of even the lowest-income households that there is no basis for singling it out for subsidization—for all households, rural households, or just low-income households. In many developed countries, low-income households spend as much on alcohol, tobacco, or products for personal care (toiletries and cosmetics) as on telephone service. If virtually all households in these countries would opt for telephone service anyway, why is a policy of cross-subsidy necessary?

An important characteristic that distinguishes telephone service in most countries from the services of other household durables, however, is that the monthly cost of using the service (that is, calling) exceeds the monthly fee for access to it, and often by unpredictable amounts. This is not true for most other durables, whose monthly usage costs are largely known in advance with little variance. Even air conditioning and heating costs can be predicted with some accuracy although they vary with the weather. Telephony is unique in placing unpredictable burdens on households owing to the variance in monthly calling and, in some cases, to the difficulty of preventing family members, friends, or others from using the home's telephone.

This unique nature of telephony clearly leads to two policy prescriptions. First, any attempt to pay for access through supracompetitive prices for calling is likely to be counterproductive because it places undue burdens on some households and eventually leads some households to face loss of service because of the difficulty in paying for the high costs of calling.[17] This may be one reason why Jerry Hausman, Timothy Tardiff, and Andrew Belinfante found that the demand for access is inversely related to long-distance rates.[18] Second, this difficulty in predicting calling expenses suggests that innovative policies of providing prepaid calling packages, such as debit cards, could be helpful in ensuring universality of telephone service.

3 | *Who Pays for Telephone Service?*

In many countries, the residential customer typically buys local telephone service and long-distance service from different suppliers. The local telephone company provides the line to the residence, connects local calls, offers long-distance service over a limited nearby area, and supplies a variety of "vertical services," such as call waiting, messaging, and number identification. In the United States and Canada, most residential service is offered with unlimited local calling—in other words, local calls are priced at zero, a price that is surely below cost during peak usage. Furthermore, residential lines and even some business lines are priced below cost, but long-distance service and the vertical services are generally priced above cost. Traditionally all such services have been heavily regulated but protected to varying degrees from entry by the regulators. In European countries, however, local calls are generally priced substantially above their marginal cost, usually at prices that range from ten cents to twenty cents (U.S. dollars) for three minutes.[1] (See table 1-3 in chapter 1.)

Despite wide differences in local access and usage pricing and similarly wide variation in long-distance rates, consumer expenditure patterns on telephone service are remarkably similar across countries. High-income consumers typically spend two to three times as much as low-income consumers on telephone service. Equally important, many low-income consumers spend far more on telephone service than a large number of high-income consumers precisely because of the policies of keeping calling charges high to cross subsidize monthly connection charges.

In this chapter, we analyze the burden of these policies on households across income levels in three countries with very different universal-service policies: the United States, Canada, and the United Kingdom. The United States, through its state regulatory commissions, keeps local residential rates below business rates, generally requires rural rates to be below urban rates, and usually requires local calling charges to be zero. Canada follows a similar policy and has traditionally kept local residential rates even below U.S. rates. Though both countries have now opened long-distance services to competition, each maintains a system of "contributions" from long-distance services to defray the cost of local service through access charges levied on each long-distance call. During the most recent period for which we have Canadian household expenditure data (1992), however, the long-distance market was not open to competition; therefore, Canada serves as the example of the most regulated market in the three countries analyzed in this chapter. The United Kingdom, however, maintains a uniform, national residential connection charge (22 pounds or $35.00 per quarter in 1998), but levies local calling charges of up to $0.20 per three-minute call. Long-distance service is open to competition in the United Kingdom, but rates are generally assumed to still be somewhat above incremental cost, despite the absence of an explicit contribution charge in intercarrier access charges to cross subsidize local connections.

The United States

In the United States, long-distance service outside the local Bell companies' local access and transport areas (LATAs) is provided by national carriers (AT&T, Sprint, MCI, and so on) or regional carriers. These carriers must pay the local companies access charges to connect their calls. Because these connection charges are designed by regulators to recover 25 percent of the local companies' fixed (non-traffic-sensitive) costs, these charges averaged three cents a minute on each end of the call or six cents a minute for a normal voice call in 1996, even though the actual cost of delivering these calls to and from the long-distance carriers is perhaps one-half to one cent a conversation minute.[2] These charges accounted for about 33 percent of the total price of a call minute in 1996.[3] The difference between these access rates and the cost of originating and terminating a long-distance call—about five cents a minute—is simply a transfer or "subsidy" from long-distance to local service.[4]

Besides the per minute access charges, long-distance carriers were also assessed nearly $6.50 per subscriber line per year in 1996 to subsidize low-income and rural subscribers. Less than $1.20 of these charges were directed toward state Lifeline and Link-Up programs that subsidize monthly line rentals or new connections (installation charges) for low-income subscribers. The remainder—or about $800 million a year—went into a "high-cost" fund for rural telephone carriers.[5]

Finally, state regulators are responsible for rate structures for intrastate services that depart substantially from cost-based rates. Residential rates for local service are typically less than half the rates charged to small and medium-size businesses even though the cost of residential service is typically little different from that of business service.[6] The monthly rates for local service typically decline slowly as one moves from center cities in large urban areas to the suburbs and into rural areas even though the cost of extending such service rises significantly with declining population density. In some states, regulators have allowed a uniform pricing policy for local service across the state, a movement in the right direction, but no state requires rates to rise to reflect the additional costs of extending wires to more remote subscribers.[7] We analyze these implicit transfers from urban to rural areas more fully in a later chapter. Finally, intrastate, intra-LATA rates are also generally above cost because of the absence of intra-LATA competition in most states before the passage of the 1996 Telecommunications Act.

Household Expenditures by Type of Service

Until recently, we had little detailed data on the distribution of telephone expenditures across U.S. households. As a result, we could not measure with precision the effects of the regulatory pricing strategy on households of different income groups or in different locations. To remedy this deficiency, a private market-research firm has recently developed a stratified random sample of approximately 10,000 households' expenditures on local and long-distance telephone services as well as a variety of other services that it offers commercially to telecommunications carriers and other market participants.[8] Their 1996 data are used for this research.

Figure 3-1. *Average Monthly U.S. Household Telephone Expenditures, 1996*

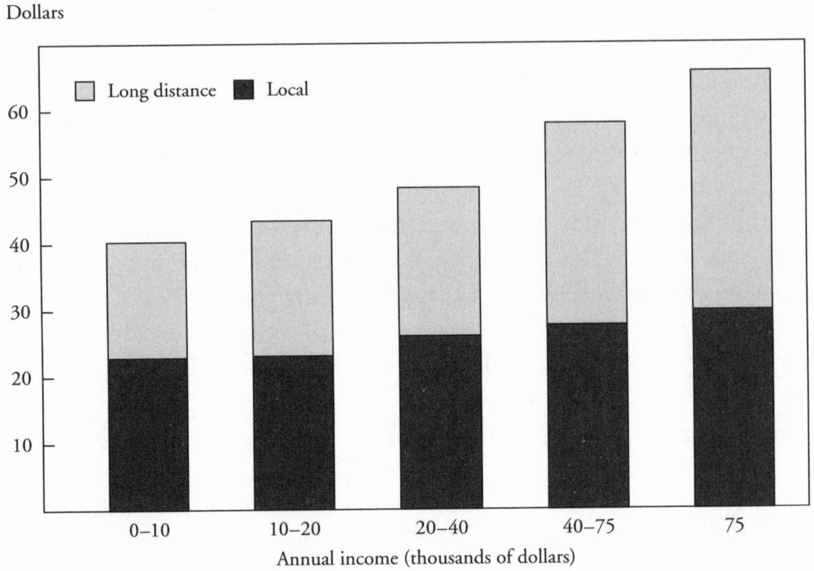

Dollars

Annual income (thousands of dollars)

Source: PNR and Associates, *Bill Harvesting Survey III* (Jenkintown, Pa., 1996).

We have aggregated these data into five income groups. They provide some rather surprising initial conclusions about the effects of universal policies.

First, in every income category, the average long-distance bill is a rather large share of total telephone expenditures. Even in the lowest-income households, those with less than $10,000 a year in annual income, 42.5 percent of the average bill is for long-distance calls (figure 3-1). Indeed, every household income class above $30,000 a year spends more on long-distance services than on all local services, including vertical services—call waiting, voice messaging, and so on.[9] Long-distance calling is not simply an indulgence of the rich.

Second, in each income category there is enormous variance in the number of long-distance calls each month. The top 10 percent of households with incomes below $10,000 spent more than $80 on long-distance calls in our sample month (table 3-1). Any attempt to keep monthly bills low by charging them more for long-distance calls is surely not a desirable redistribution of income.

Third, and surprisingly, half of high-income households—those with more than $75,000 in annual income—had long-distance bills below $25

Table 3-1. *Average Monthly U.S. Household Long-Distance Outlays, by Income Decile, 1996*
Dollars

Decile[a]	Less than $10,000	$10,000– $20,000	$20,000– $40,000	$40,000– $75,000	$75,000 or more
Lowest	0	0	0	0.18	0.63
Second	0	0.36	1.01	2.90	4.93
Third	0.86	2.14	3.66	7.22	9.68
Fourth	3.13	5.33	7.27	11.83	15.26
Fifth	5.80	8.96	11.32	16.74	21.06
Sixth	9.35	13.10	15.71	22.37	27.75
Seventh	14.56	18.21	21.76	29.50	37.28
Eighth	20.83	25.26	29.34	39.01	49.37
Ninth	31.91	37.90	42.81	54.60	67.36
Tenth	83.72	87.26	88.85	118.18	130.92
Average	17.02	19.84	22.16	30.25	36.42

Source: PNR and Associates, *Bill Harvesting III* (Jenkintown, Pa., 1996).
a. Decile indicates level of monthly long-distance spending.

a month. As a result, they paid less to the cause of universal service than did about 30 percent of the poorest households.

Finally, any universal-service support of residential lines is absorbed disproportionately by higher-income households who lease more than one line. There were about 113 million residential lines but only 95 million telephone households in 1996 because many households had two, three, or more lines to accommodate numerous family members, fax machines, and computer modems.[10] The incremental cost of second lines is generally lower than the cost of primary lines, but the rates for these second lines are still below their incremental costs in many areas. The higher-income households are clearly the most intensive users of such lines, as figure 3-1 shows. Their local telephone bills averaged about $30, even though the average residential telephone line costs only about $20 a month, in part because they leased more lines than did those in the lower-income classes.[11]

Telephone Subscription by Income Class

Given that many lower-income households consume ample long-distance service, it is surely not equitable to require these heavy long-distance

Table 3-2. *U.S. Telephone Penetration, by Nominal Income Class, Selected Years*

Percent

Annual income	1984	1990	1996
Less than $10,000	80.1	82.9	85.4
$10,000–$19,999	90.8	91.9	93.0
$20,000–$29,999	95.9	96.3	96.5
$30,000–$39,999	98.3	98.4	97.6
$40,000 or more	98.8	99.0	98.5
All households	91.8	93.4	93.9

Source: Alexander Belinfante, *Telephone Penetration by Income by State*, Industry Analysis Division, Common Carrier Bureau (Federal Communications Commission, February 1997), table 2.

users to subsidize local service for all income classes, particularly those who use little long-distance service. But the striking constancy of household spending on local service across incomes, shown in figure 3-1, demonstrates that the elaborate universal-service pricing system erected by regulators of telephone service has not led to lower local rates solely for lower-income households. All local residential rates and particularly all local rural residential rates are kept artificially low by regulators, but a substantial share of the cost of this policy is paid for by low-income households through elevated long-distance charges.[12]

A key issue is whether there is any need to keep rates for telephone connections for low-income households below cost to ensure that these households remain on the telephone network. In this chapter, we simply note that low-income telephone penetration in the United States has been rising more rapidly than has the penetration for higher-income households, which obviously have almost 100 percent subscription rates. Table 3-2 displays the trends in telephone subscribership across income levels for the 1984–96 period. Because the data in table 3-2 are displayed for categories of nominal income, they understate the degree to which lower-income households have increasingly connected to telephone service. In 1996 a nominal income of $15,000 was equivalent in real terms to a nominal income of $10,000 in 1984. Therefore, the increase in telephone subscribership among persons with real incomes of less than $10,000 has undoubtedly been far greater than the 5.3 percentage point gain shown in table 3-2. But even table 3-2 shows that the telephone has now become almost ubiquitous for households with incomes above $20,000.

Given the federal Lifeline and Link-Up subsidy programs that have existed for ten years or more, all but a few states have some form of subsidy program directed at various categories of low-income households. As explained in chapter 1, the Lifeline program provides matching funds for state programs that reduce the monthly charge for eligible households, while the Link-Up program provides matching funds for reducing the installation charges for these households. Both programs are funded from taxes on long-distance services, but Lifeline received about eight times the federal funding that was directed to the Link-Up program in 1996.

At best only a modest possibility exists that subsidies for monthly telephone connection charges are very successful in increasing subscribership among low-income households. As reported in chapter 1, interviews and anecdotal evidence suggest that a large share of the low-income households without telephone service currently do not subscribe because they have run up large long-distance bills in previous months. When they are unable to pay these long-distance charges, their entire telephone service is disconnected. Lower local monthly rates would not ameliorate their condition, but lower installation charges might. Thus a much more significant case exists for Link-Up subsidies than for the Lifeline program.[13]

Rural versus Urban Subscribers

The current U.S. universal-service system is often defended as necessary to promote telephone subscription among rural households, who are pictured as far poorer than their city brethren. Average household income is somewhat lower in rural areas than in urban areas (figure 3-2), but some of this differential is probably offset by the lower cost of living in rural areas. Nevertheless, providing below-cost telephone access to "high-cost" rural areas may be defensible if such a policy is directed at low-income households in these areas. Unfortunately, the current system of implicitly taxing all long-distance services to provide general below-cost rural service to low-income and higher-income households alike means significant income transfer among rural households.

If "rural" is defined as all areas outside metropolitan statistical areas (MSAs)—accounting for 20.3 percent of the U.S. population in 1990—we can show that the average local telephone bills of lower-income rural households are nearly identical to those of lower-income households in MSAs (figure 3-3), even though the cost of extending lines in these rural areas is clearly much greater than in urban areas. However, rural house-

Figure 3-2. *U.S. Income Distribution, Urban (MSA) versus Rural (Non-MSA) Households, 1990*

Cumulative share of households

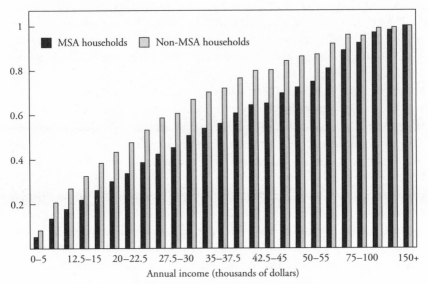

Annual income (thousands of dollars)

Source: 1990 Census data from Geolytics, *Census CD* (East Brunswick, N.J., 1996).

holds spend more on long-distance service than their urban equivalents at every income level (figure 3-4). The distribution of long-distance expenditures is just as skewed in rural areas as in urban areas.[14] Finally, figure 3-5 shows the average long-distance bill in rural and urban areas for households arrayed by increasing levels of spending.

Given these patterns, it is clear that the current practice of using high long-distance access charges to keep local rates artificially low results in substantial transfers from heavy rural long-distance users to light long-distance users—and even to light long-distance users in urban areas.[15] Part of the reason for the transfer is that rural households pay higher long-distance rates than do urban households. In 1996 rural residences paid an average inter-LATA rate of nineteen cents a minute while urban residences paid only seventeen and a half cents a minute. Similarly, rural residences paid an average intra-LATA rate of sixteen cents a minute while urban residences paid only twelve cents a minute, and these rates are regulated by the same state authorities that control the structure of local rates. Because of their location, rural households use intra-LATA services more intensively

Figure 3-3. *Average Monthly Local Telephone Bill, Urban (MSA) versus Rural (Non-MSA) Households, 1996*

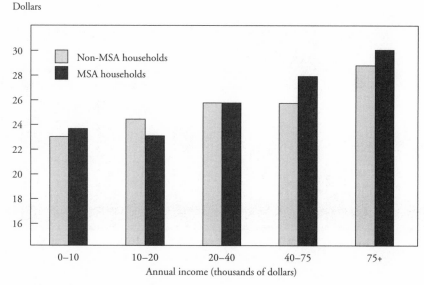

Dollars

Annual income (thousands of dollars)

Source: PNR and Associates, *Bill Harvesting Survey III.*

than do urban households. Therefore, state regulators essentially tax those telephone subscribers making large numbers of the shorter, in-state long-distance calls to help finance the costs of those who do not.

Canada

The Canadian telephone industry was organized as a series of vertically integrated monopolies until the Canadian Radio-Television and Telecommunications Commission (CRTC) opened the long-distance market to competition in 1992. Furthermore, before 1992, several provinces operated state-owned telecommunications monopolies. Ontario and Quebec were served principally by Bell Canada, a private company, which was also the largest long-distance carrier in Canada.

The telephone rate structure has been more distorted in Canada than in the United States. Long-distance rates had been allowed to remain very high before liberalization, and local rates were even lower than those in the United States and often embraced larger local calling areas.[16] When liber-

Figure 3-4. *Average Monthly Long-Distance Bill, Urban (MSA) versus Rural (Non-MSA) Households, 1996*

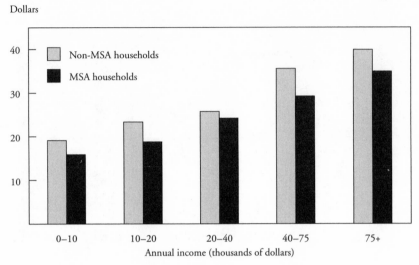

Dollars

Source: PNR and Associates, *Bill Harvesting Survey III.*

Figure 3-5. *Distribution of Monthly Long-Distance Bills, Urban (MSA) versus Rural (Non-MSA) Households, 1996*

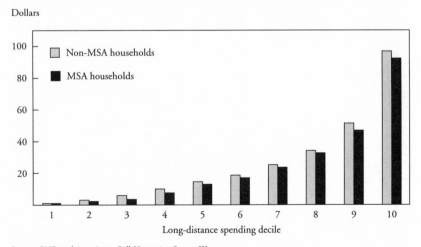

Dollars

Source: PNR and Associates, *Bill Harvesting Survey III.*

Table 3-3. *Average Annual Telephone Expenditures in Canadian and U.S. Households, by Income, 1992*

U.S. dollars

Annual income	Local basic charge (Canada)	Long-distance (Canada)	Total telephone (Canada)	Total telephone (U.S.)
Less than 5,000	141	133	284	425
5,000–9,999	174	125	281	417
10,000–14,999	179	196	370	528
15,000–19,999	185	237	424	548
20,000–29,999	189	272	468	614
30,000–39,999	198	308	512	659
40,000–49,999	203	325	536	697
50,000–69,999	212	367	591	768
70,000 or more	231	449	703	917

Sources: Statistics Canada, *Family Expenditure in Canada 1992;* and Bureau of Labor Statistics, *Consumer Expenditure Survey, 1992* (Department of Labor, 1992).

alization occurred in 1992, the CRTC attempted a mild rebalancing of rates by establishing a Cdn$6 a month increase in local rates through a subscriber line charge. Even though this increase was to be phased in over three years, the political opposition was so strong that the Cabinet suspended it. In 1995 the subscriber line charges were once again imposed, but they were not to be offset by lower calling charges.

Our data on Canadian household expenditures for telephone service are for 1992 and thus antedate the liberalization of long-distance services. Nevertheless, the distribution of telephone expenditures across income levels seems noticeably similar to those found in the United States for the same year. The data in table 3-3 are drawn from each country's consumer expenditure surveys, but the U.S. data include cellular services while the Canadian data do not.

At the lower income levels, at least $100 of the $140 difference between the U.S. and Canadian expenditures is attributable to differences in local charges.[17] At the higher income levels, however, the difference rises to $200 a year, mostly because of the inclusion of cellular expenditures in the U.S. data. Because the United States has had far lower long-distance rates, there is much more long-distance calling in the United States than in Canada. In 1992, for example, the number of national long-distance

Table 3-4. *Average Annual Household Spending on Telephone Services in the United Kingdom, by Income, 1995*
U.S. dollars

Income decile	Local line rental (one line)	Local and long-distance calls and other services	Total telephone expenditure
Lowest	158	52	210
Second	158	120	278
Third	158	164	322
Fourth	158	211	369
Fifth	158	239	397
Sixth	158	249	404
Seventh	158	283	441
Eighth	158	311	469
Ninth	158	364	532
Highest	158	474	624

Source: United Kingdom Office for National Statistics, *Family Expenditure Survey, 1995–96.*

calls per line was 500 in the United States but only 200 in Canada.[18] Despite these differences in rates, however, overall household spending on long-distance services was remarkably similar to that in the United States, undoubtedly reflecting the fact that the price-elasticity demand for long-distance services is not much below unity in Canada.

The United Kingdom

Few of the other OECD countries have moved as far toward liberalizing their telephone sector as have the United States and Canada. Before 1998, only New Zealand, Finland, Sweden, and the United Kingdom had opened their long-distance and local markets to competition. Liberalization is now spreading because the European Union established January 1998 as the deadline for liberalization for most of its member countries. As we have seen, all of these countries have some form of universal-service policy that keeps local connection rates low while allowing their carriers to charge above-cost rates for long-distance services and local calls.

The data on U.K. household spending on telephone service by income decile are shown in table 3-4. Note that the lowest-income households spend much less than their U.S. counterparts (table 3-3) but about the same as Canadian households. The reason for these differences is almost entirely due to differences in local charges. Canadian local rates are far below U.S. local rates, though similarly distorted between urban and rural areas. The United Kingdom, however, has uniform national "line-rental" rates of about $13 a month, or about two-thirds of the U.S. average rate.

The second column in table 3-4 shows U.K. household expenditures on all other (noncellular) telephone services, including local calls, second lines, and vertical services. Consumers in the United Kingdom must pay for each local call; hence, these calls add greatly to household expenditures. Long-distance (national) calls cost only about ten cents a minute, much less than the average rates in the United States or Canada.[19]

Household Spending on Telephone Services in the Three Countries

Despite the very large differences in universal-service and other regulatory policies across these three countries, the distribution of household expenditures across income levels is extremely similar. The average expenditures in each of our five income categories are shown in table 3-5. Clearly, the United States has the highest average spending in every income category, and the United Kingdom has the lowest. Despite very different universal-service policies and long-distance regimes, there are virtually no differences in average long-distance spending across the three countries. (Recall, however, that the U.K. long-distance spending includes expenditures on local calls.) This remarkable similarity in long-distance expenditure patterns occurs even though the price of long-distance services varied enormously across the three countries in the years covered—from about ten cents a minute in the United Kingdom to seventeen cents a minute in the United States to about thirty cents a minute in Canada.[20] Finally, the similarity extends to the distribution of expenditures within each income category. Figures 3-6 through 3-10 show that the United States and Canada share almost identically skewed distributions in household long-distance expenditures in all but the lowest-income categories. Indeed, Canada has a somewhat more skewed distribution in most of the higher-income categories, undoubtedly because of its much higher long-distance rates in 1992. The United Kingdom, with the lowest long-distance rates and the smallest geographical area of the three countries, has a somewhat less skewed distribution of household spending on long-distance services, but its distribution is remarkably close to that of Canada's distribution even

Table 3-5. *Average Monthly Household Expenditures on Telephone Service (Excluding Cellular), by Income*
U.S. dollars

Annual income	Canada (1992)			United Kingdom (1995)			United States (1996)		
	Local service	*Long-distance*	*Total telephone*	*Local service*	*Long-distance and other*	*Total telephone*	*Local service*	*Long-distance*	*Total telephone*
Less than 10,000	12.91	9.81	22.72	13.17	16.52	29.69	23.04	17.02	40.06
10,000–20,000	14.63	17.44	32.07	13.17	19.50	32.67	23.24	20.04	43.28
20,000–40,000	15.78	23.73	39.51	13.17	22.98	36.15	25.54	22.32	47.86
40,000–75,000	17.00	28.92	45.92	13.17	28.39	41.56	27.26	30.25	57.51
75,000 or more	19.52	38.17	57.69	13.17	37.24	50.41	29.49	35.85	65.34

Sources: For Canada, Statistics Canada, *Family Expenditure in Canada, 1992*; for United Kingdom, U.K. Office for National Statistics, *Family Expenditure Survey, 1995–96*; and for United States, PNR and Associates, *Bill Harvesting Survey III*.

Figure 3-6. *Monthly Long-Distance Spending: Household Income Less Than $10,000*

U.S. dollars

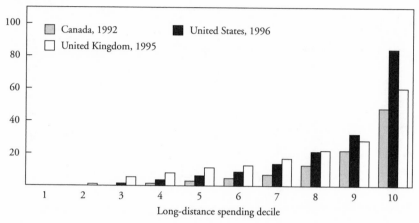

Long-distance spending decile

Source: See text.

Figure 3-7. *Monthly Long-Distance Spending: Household Income $10,000–$20,000*

U.S. dollars

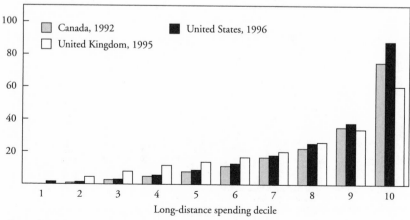

Long-distance spending decile

Source: See text.

Figure 3-8. *Monthly Long-Distance Spending: Household Income $20,000–$40,000*

U.S. dollars

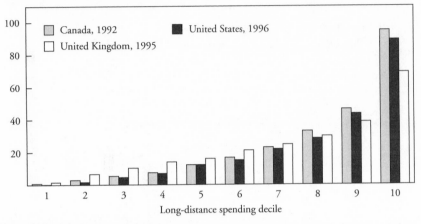

Long-distance spending decile

Source: See text.

Figure 3-9. *Monthly Long-Distance Spending: Household Income $40,000–$75,000*

U.S. dollars

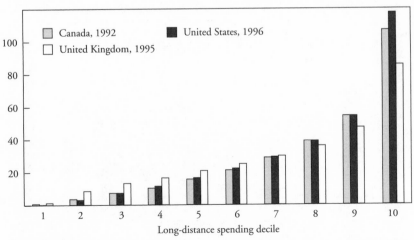

Long-distance spending decile

Source: See text.

Figure 3-10. *Monthly Long-Distance Spending: Household Income above $75,000*

U.S. dollars

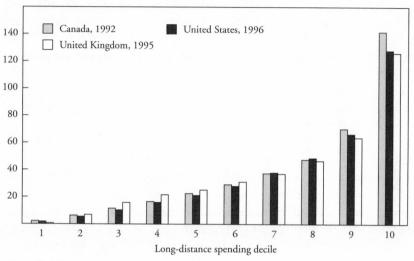

Source: See text.

though the United Kingdom's 1995 long-distance rates were no more than 40 percent of Canada's 1992 rates.

We conclude from this comparison of household spending patterns that different universal-service policies across the three countries certainly influence the amount households spend to connect to the telephone network. However, differences in the structure of rates and differences in universal-service policies across the three countries have very little effect on total household spending on long-distance (national) calls. Indeed, it appears that these differences are largely absorbed in differences in the extent of long-distance calling. Thus, policies designed to subsidize connections to the network may not have major effects on the number of households that choose to subscribe, but they surely have major effects on the amount of network usage by all households.

The Welfare Consequences of High Long-Distance Rates

In recent years, the price of long-distance services has fallen in all three of the countries whose rates we analyze in this section. Nevertheless, in each country the price of long-distance service is still above its long-run competitive equilibrium in part because of universal-service policies. The United Kingdom has perhaps gone the farthest toward rebalancing rates toward economic costs, but the United States and Canada continue to allow long-distance rates to provide "contributions" to local rates.[21] Because we have the most complete data for the United States, we now investigate the welfare and income-distribution effects of reducing long-distance rates by reducing access charges and raising local rates accordingly. In a subsequent chapter, we examine the implications of several alternatives to the current U.S. universal-service policy, including recent proposals to substitute a tax on telecom revenues for the current system of implicit subsidies.

The average price paid for long-distance service in the United States is strikingly constant across income levels. In 1996 low-income households paid about fourteen cents a minute for the shorter intra-LATA calls provided mainly by their local telephone company. High-income households paid an average of thirteen cents a minute.[22] Similarly, for the longer inter-LATA calls, low-income and high-income households paid about the same price—eighteen cents a minute—although the higher-income households tend to make calls that average slightly more than 600 miles while low-income households average about 500 miles.

Were regulators to have eliminated the implicit support flowing from residential long-distance calls to local services in 1996, they would essentially have reduced access charges by $0.05 a minute.[23] This reduction, in turn, would have reduced long-distance rates by about the same amount—or by 30 percent. If this reduction were to occur for residential customers, the local companies would suffer an immediate loss of $12.5 billion on the roughly 250 billion residential calls, or about $110 per residential line each year. Since lower long-distance rates would stimulate greater calling, the net loss to local companies would likely be about $10.5 billion, or $93 per line per year.[24] At the same time, the increase in local rates would reduce the number of subscribers by a few percentage points, but most of those disconnecting would likely be customers that are now unprofitable. Thus, a $7.00 per month increase in local rates would likely be sufficient to recover the lost access revenues. Put another way, the support flowing from residential long-distance to residential local service was about $7.00 per month per line in 1996.

What if the Federal Communications Commission (FCC) and the state regulators had attempted to rebalance at least residential long-distance and local rates by reducing the former by $0.05 a minute and raising

Figure 3-11. *Average Monthly Expenditures after Repricing, 1996*

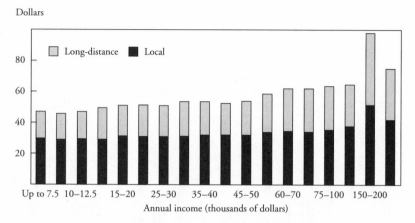

Source: Authors' calculations based on PNR and Associates, *Bill Harvesting Survey III.*

the latter by $7.00 a month? Would "consumers" have suffered? Would low-income consumers have suffered more acutely than high-income consumers? Figure 3-11 provides the bare elements of an answer. Comparing figures 3-1 and 3-11 reveals surprisingly little average change in telephone bills across consumer groups.

Figure 3-12 shows the change in total telephone spending per month as a result of this "drastic" rebalancing. No income class would have suffered as much as a $5.50 average increase in its monthly bill. But the increase in consumer welfare—the value of telephone service to the consumer—is more than the increase in spending for all but the three lowest-income classes, and even these lowest-income classes suffer only an average loss of between $0.39 and $0.79 a month per household, or $4.68 to $9.48 a year. For instance, those with annual incomes between $7,500 and $10,000 would suffer losses equal to about 0.1 percent of their annual income. On average, each household would gain more than $15.00 a year, for a total gain to the economy of more than $1.5 billion a year.[25]

The Effects of Rate Rebalancing by Income Class

The results shown in figures 3-11 and 3-12 fail to come to grips with the substantial differences in long-distance spending within income classes. The average residential long-distance bill in the sample month was $25;

Figure 3-12. *Monthly Effect of Repricing on Households, 1996*

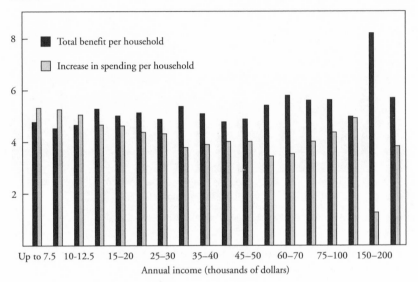

Dollars

Annual income (thousands of dollars)

■ Total benefit per household

□ Increase in spending per household

Up to 7.5   10-12.5   15–20   25–30   35–40   45–50   60–70   75–100   150–200

Source: Authors' calculations based on PNR and Associates, *Bill Harvesting Survey III.*

however, as table 3-1 shows, most households in every income group spent less than $25.[26] This skewness in the distribution of long-distance calling is well recognized within the industry, but these data show that it exists in every income category. It may also help to explain why the universal-service policy of keeping local rates below cost by raising the price of long-distance services is politically popular. One-third of all households account for more than half of residential long-distance spending, which in turn accounts for only 47 percent of all long-distance expenditures. Business spending on long-distance accounts for the other 53 percent. Thus, two-thirds of the nation's residential consumers account for less than one-fourth of total long-distance spending.

The impacts of local/long-distance rate rebalancing on each of the five income classes shown in table 3-1 may be seen in figures 3-13 through 3-17, which array households in terms of their monthly long-distance bills. In the two lowest-income classes, each decile except for the highest experiences an increase in its total monthly telephone bill from the repricing of local and long-distance service. Additionally, the three highest deciles in these two groups (less than $20,000 in annual income) realize an improve-

Figure 3-13. *Monthly Effect of Repricing on Households with Annual Income under $10,000, 1996*

Dollars

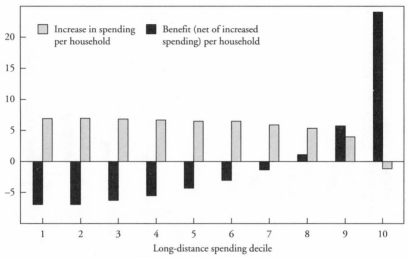

Long-distance spending decile

Source: Authors' calculations based on PNR and Associates, *Bill Harvesting Survey III.*

Figure 3-14. *Monthly Effect of Repricing on Households with Annual Income $10,000–$20,000, 1996*

Dollars

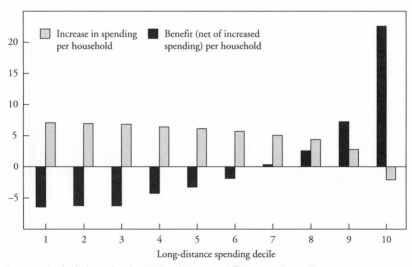

Long-distance spending decile

Source: Authors' calculations based on PNR and Associates, *Bill Harvesting Survey III.*

Figure 3-15. *Monthly Effect of Repricing on Households with Annual Income $20,000–$40,000, 1996*

Dollars

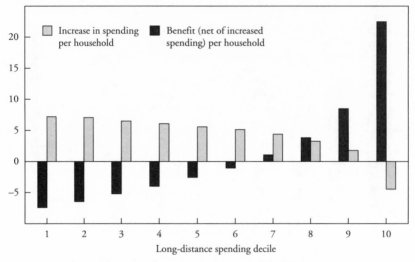

Long-distance spending decile

Source: Authors' calculations based on PNR and Associates, *Bill Harvesting Survey III.*

Figure 3-16. *Monthly Effect of Repricing on Households with Annual Income $40,000–$75,000, 1996*

Dollars

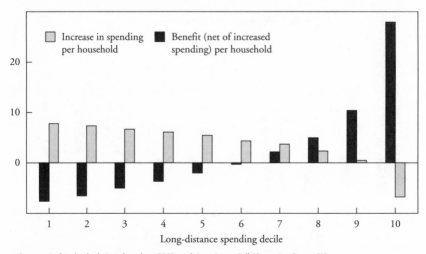

Long-distance spending decile

Source: Authors' calculations based on PNR and Associates, *Bill Harvesting Survey III.*

Figure 3-17. *Monthly Effect of Repricing on Households with Annual Income above $75,000, 1996*

Dollars

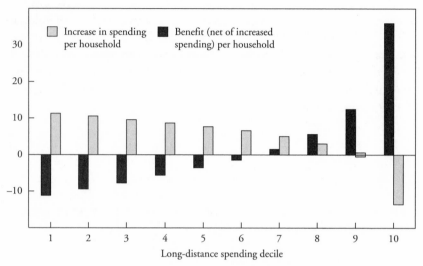

Long-distance spending decile

Source: Authors' calculations based on PNR and Associates, *Bill Harvesting Survey III*.

ment in their economic welfare from their increased long-distance calling that is facilitated by lower access charges.

In every other income category, the top 40 percent of households in terms of long-distance expenditure gain while the bottom 60 percent suffer some losses. Ironically, the largest losers in our analysis are wealthy households with very little long-distance spending because we assume that households with $75,000 in annual income or more have an average of 1.5 local lines per residence. Once again, every income class other than the lowest-income class gains on average, but there are very large gains from rebalancing among the heaviest long-distance users and generally moderate losses for the rest, owing to the increase of local rates toward cost.

Conclusion

Clearly, a policy to hold local rates low by raising long-distance rates far above long-run incremental cost is very inefficient. Consumers on average would gain from a relaxation of this "consumerist" universal-service policy in most countries that practice it. Equally important, in the three countries that we have studied with care, the distribution of long-distance calling is extremely skewed in every income category. As a result, the policy of implicitly supporting local rates from long-distance service rates inevitably transfers income from some poor households to some rich ones even though average residential spending on long distance increases with income. In a later chapter, we show that this policy, as practiced in the United States, also penalizes rural subscribers in the most rural states because these subscribers are forced to pay the highest intrastate long-distance rates.

4

"Universal" Service in Other Regulated Sectors in the United States

The average U.S. household receives many services from regulated public utility companies. Most of these services are delivered through network facilities that exhibit many of the economies of fill and scale that are present in modern telephony and that arguably create "natural monopoly" conditions. Many, such as water and sewage, may also generate externalities. Surely, each of us would benefit from our neighbors using sanitary water and sewage services. And each of these services is likely to be more expensive to deliver to rural homes than to most urban locations. But do regulators generally pursue "universal service" policies, that is, create large cross-subsidies between businesses and residences and between urban and rural areas? This chapter investigates this question for a number of such U.S. services, including electricity, natural gas, and cable television.

We have seen that telephone service accounts for but a small share of the average consumer's budget and that this share declines slowly with total household spending.[1] But telephony accounts for only about one-third of total household expenditures on utility services (table 4-1). In 1995 electricity accounted for 2.5 percent of total expenditures for the average household; telephony accounted for 2.1 percent of household expenditures. The data in table 4-1 show a remarkably stable relationship in the relative distri-

Table 4-1. *Consumer Spending on "Utilities" as a Share of Total U.S. Household Expenditures, 1995*

Percent

Service	All households	Annual income								
		Less than $5,000	$5,000–$9,999	$10,000–$14,999	$15,000–$19,999	$20,000–$29,999	$30,000–$39,999	$40,000–$49,999	$50,000–$69,999	$70,000 or more
Utilities, fuels, and public services	6.5	9.4	10.3	9.2	8.4	7.6	6.8	6.1	5.5	4.6
Electricity	2.5	3.7	4.1	3.7	3.3	3.1	2.7	2.3	2.2	1.8
Natural gas	0.8	1.2	1.3	1.2	1.0	0.9	0.8	0.8	0.6	0.6
Fuel oil and other fuels	0.3	0.2	0.5	0.4	0.3	0.4	0.2	0.2	0.2	0.2
Telephone	2.1	3.3	3.5	2.9	2.8	2.5	2.3	2.0	1.8	1.5
Water and other public services	0.8	1.0	1.0	1.0	1.0	0.8	0.8	0.8	0.7	0.6

Source: Bureau of Labor Statistics, *Consumer Expenditure Survey 1995* (Department of Labor, 1995), table 2.

bution of consumer expenditures across electricity, fuel oil and natural gas, and telephone services as income rises. Regardless of income, telephone services account for only about one-third of household purchases of public utility services. Surely, any equity concerns in pricing telephone services also exist for these other essential utility services such as water, electricity, or fossil fuels for heating. Thus, the case for a universal service policy, if it exists, should apply to all such regulated utilities. We shall see, however, that telephone is the only sector regulated in this fashion.

Nor has this expenditure pattern changed much since 1984.[2] In 1984 households in all income categories devoted a larger relative share of their income to electricity, natural gas, and fuel oil because fossil fuel and electricity prices were higher in real terms in the early 1980s. But the ratio of spending on electricity to purchases of telephone services did not vary much across income classes in 1984 either. At that time, expenditures on electricity accounted for 1.44 times the average expenditure on telephone service, and this ratio varied only from 1.32 to 1.51 across the entire distribution of income.

Electricity

There is perhaps no household public utility service as "essential" as electric service. One can imagine a modern household without a telephone, but attempting to operate a home without electricity would create much greater difficulties. Lighting fixtures, refrigerators, toasters, radios, television sets, computers, and even many heating systems are driven by electricity. Indeed, the average U.S. household spends 20 percent more on electricity than on telephone services.[3]

Regulation

Like telephony, electricity is regulated in the United States by federal and state authorities. The Federal Energy Regulatory Commission (FERC) regulates the interstate distribution of electricity while state commissions regulate intrastate generation, distribution, and sales of electricity. In addition, the Rural Electrification Administration (REA) distributes subsidies to rural cooperatives who collectively account for about 5 percent of the nation's power. The REA also administers the direct and indirect federal loan subsidies offered to rural telephone companies by the federal government. Finally, the federal government subsidizes electric power through a variety of public power programs, such as the Bonneville Power Administration (BPA) and the Tennessee Valley Authority (TVA), who account for about 8 percent of the country's electricity.[4] In short, the opportunities for developing universal service programs to cross-subsidize high-cost or low-income consumers are at least as great for electricity as for telephony.

Electricity Subsidy Programs

The subsidy programs administered by the federal government affect less than 15 percent of the nation's electricity generation. Subsidies to about 900 rural cooperatives, while substantial, affect no more than 8.5 percent of revenue from power sales to ultimate consumers. The federal power projects, such as TVA and BPA, provide low-cost power to residents in the Northwest and South. There are also a variety of small, publicly owned municipal electric companies that distribute—but typically do not generate—electric power. These publicly owned utilities account for 9.5 percent of generation and 14 percent of electricity sales.

The rural electric subsidies take the form of low-interest-rate loans. Before 1974 the REA extended these loans at an interest rate of 2 percent; since that time, these loans have carried a 5 percent interest rate. The program is administered today by the Rural Utilities Service of the Department of Agriculture, which issues very few new loans to rural electric cooperatives. The value of the subsidy in 1990 was estimated to be $1.14 billion a year when evaluated at investor-owned utility borrowing rates.[5] Given that these cooperatives serve about 11.5 million customers, most of which are residences or farms, the average annual value of the subsidy was $100 per customer in 1990.

Electricity Rates

We begin with an analysis of residential and commercial rates across the states. The most recent year for which the Energy Information Administration (EIA) provides comprehensive data is 1998. In that year, the average residential rate—measured in revenue per unit of electricity consumed—was 8.26 cents per kilowatt hour (kWh).[6] Not surprisingly, the states with the lowest residential rates were Idaho, Washington, Oregon, and Tennessee, states with access to low-cost power from federal power projects (table 4-2). The states with the highest rates were New York, California, and the New England states, states with very different economies. The low-rate

Table 4-2. *Average Residential and Commercial Electricity Rates, Selected States, 1998*
Revenues (cents) per kilowatt hour

State	Residential rate	Commercial rate
New Hampshire	13.92	11.64
New York	13.66	11.63
Maine	13.02	10.33
New Jersey	11.39	10.09
California	10.60	9.66
Illinois	9.85	7.77
Ohio	8.70	7.67
North Carolina	8.01	6.35
Florida	7.89	6.38
Texas	7.65	6.57
Colorado	7.45	5.67
Utah	6.84	5.71
Tennessee	6.32	6.28
Oregon	5.82	5.00
Idaho	5.28	4.34
Washington	5.03	4.81

Source: Energy Information Administration, *Electric Sales and Revenue 1998* (Department of Energy, 1999), table 12.

states had average residential rates of about 5.5 cents per kWh; the latter had rates averaging 12.5 cents per kWh. In large part these differences reflect differences in the availability of low-cost fuels and differences in state regulation. In general, those states that allowed or encouraged nuclear power now have very high rates; states with little nuclear power and considerable local low-cost fossil fuels have the lowest rates.

The EIA data are drawn from many electric utilities, serving geographic areas of different sizes and population density. Most of the large investor-owned utilities serve a large number of separate jurisdictions, but there are numerous city-owned utilities that we can match with 1990 census data for individual towns or cities to determine whether the residential rates vary systematically with population density or with other demographic characteristics. Estimating a simple linear regression of the 1998 residential revenue per kWh on population density, median income per household, and dummy variables for each geographical region, we find a direct effect of population density, suggesting that households in the

Table 4-3. *Average Revenues per kWh, by Type of U.S. Utility, 1998*
Cents per kilowatt hour

Region	Investor- owned	Publicly owned	Cooperative	Federal	All classes
New England	10.06	8.89	14.61	. . .	10.00
Middle Atlantic	9.63	8.06	9.78	. . .	9.49
East North Central	6.52	5.71	7.12	. . .	6.49
West North Central	5.96	5.46	6.54	1.41	5.93
South Atlantic	6.31	6.40	7.42	3.20	6.44
East South Central	5.13	5.76	5.81	2.81	5.27
West South Central	5.84	6.03	6.51	. . .	5.93
Mountain	5.95	6.18	5.98	2.50	5.93
Pacific Contiguous	8.23	6.22	5.06	1.80	7.26
Alaska/Hawaii	11.54	9.82	9.88	3.45	10.99
U.S. average	6.94	6.20	6.66	2.38	6.74

Source: Energy Information Administration, *Electric Sales and Revenue 1998* (Department of Energy, 1999), table 13.

more dense towns or cities pay slightly more per kWh than those in less dense areas. This effect is rather small—doubling the population density in a state of average density would raise rates only by 2 percent.

If electricity rates were based on costs, we would expect rates to be higher in rural areas because—as in telephony—the cost per customer of the distribution plant is surely higher in rural areas than in densely populated urban areas. The $100 per customer annual REA subsidy, described above, surely contributes to the perverse relationship between population density and electricity rates because it amounts to about 12 percent of the average U.S. household bill for electricity. However, some of the observed difference may be because of higher pollution-control costs in densely populated areas, which are more likely to qualify as "nonattainment" areas under EPA regulations.[7]

Unlike the cross-subsidy program in telephony, the rural electric subsidies do not come from urban electricity consumers but from the Treasury. Moreover, these subsidies have not been extended to the point where high-cost rural consumers pay significantly less for the same service than their big-city brethren. As table 4-3 shows, cooperatives realize greater revenues per kilowatt hour in most regions of the country than the average supplier of electric power. On average, cooperatives realize only about 4 percent less per kWh than do investor-owned firms and about 1 percent

Table 4-4. *Ratio of Average Residential to Average Commercial Prices, U.S. Electricity and Natural Gas, 1970–94*

Year	Electricity	Natural gas
1970	1.07	1.41
1972	1.06	1.37
1974	1.02	1.35
1976	1.01	1.20
1978	0.99	1.15
1980	0.98	1.08
1982	1.00	1.07
1984	1.00	1.10
1986	1.03	1.15
1988	1.08	1.18
1990	1.08	1.17
1992	1.09	1.20
1994	1.10	1.16

Source: Energy Information Administration, *State Energy Price and Expenditure Report 1995* (Department of Energy, 1998), tables 6, 7.

less than the average source of electric power in the United States. The average rural consumer appears to use significantly more electricity than the U.S. average, however. In 1995 subsidized rural cooperatives realized $9.93 billion from residential sales to 10.4 million residential subscribers, or about $950 per subscriber.[8] By comparison, the average U.S. household spent only $854 on electricity in 1995.[9]

Although regulators may attempt to cross-subsidize residential electricity service from the commercial or industrial electrical revenues of the same utility, such subsidies are not immediately apparent in the data. As table 4-4 shows, the average ratio of price per kWh for residential service to average kWh for commercial service is about 1.10, undoubtedly reflecting the lower cost per kWh of serving the average commercial customer (industrial rates per kWh are even lower). This ratio fell during the 1970s oil crises, perhaps because regulators found it more difficult politically to pass on large cost increases to residential customers, but after oil and natural gas prices broke in the early 1980s, the premium paid by the average residential purchaser quickly returned to 1970 levels.

We also analyzed average electricity revenues per million British thermal units (Btus) across the states. We are unable to find any statistically significant relationship between either the average residential price (revenue per million Btus) of electricity or the ratio of residential to commercial revenues per kWh across the lower forty-eight states and population density, after accounting for the price of coal and the specific effects of TVA and BPA through dummy variables for the Northwest and South Central regions of the country. Residential electricity rates are somewhat higher in high-income states, but there is no association of rates with various other political and demographic variables. Moreover, the ratio of residential to commercial rates does not vary systematically with any of these variables; the differences in this ratio appear to be largely random.

In short, our results suggest rather strongly that there is no obvious pattern of cross-subsidy between classes of customers in regulated electricity rates. Unlike local telephone service, electricity is provided to commercial users at rates below those offered residential subscribers.[10] Substantial direct subsidies flow to rural cooperatives, but these subsidies have little effect on the overall pattern of rates because these co-ops are a small part of the electricity sector, and their rates are not appreciably lower than the average rate in most states. Nevertheless, those rural consumers who are served by rural cooperatives, roughly 10.5 million households, are the beneficiaries of subsidies that amount to as much as 12 percent of their average spending on electricity. In addition, publicly owned utilities may offer somewhat lower rates than investor-owned utilities, but these lower rates do not accrue solely to residential or rural ratepayers. Thus the only major universal service policy in effect today in the U.S. electricity sector is a program of capital subsidies to rural electric cooperatives. One may debate the need for continuing these subsidies, particularly because they are not targeted to low-income households, but at least they do not distort electricity rates outside of the subsidized areas.

We do not attempt to estimate the welfare losses resulting from these subsidies because a full analysis of the distortions they create in the supply of electric power is beyond the scope of our work. Nevertheless, the $1.14 billion annual subsidy, funded from general revenues, is likely to be associated with far lower efficiency losses to the U.S. economy than is the universal service policy for telephone service.

Natural Gas

Natural gas is less of a necessity, only because heating oil and electricity are clearly substitutes as the household's source of energy for heating and cooking. But natural gas is surely an important commodity for many U.S. households, and it provides useful competition for heating oil in markets in which the distribution of heating oil may be imperfectly competitive.

Regulation

The production of natural gas was regulated throughout the 1960s and most of the 1970s with unfortunate consequences. By attempting to keep the producer's price of natural gas low, regulators only succeeded in creating a scarcity of gas.[11] When the OPEC oil crises struck in the 1970s, the demand pressures on artificially scarce natural gas intensified. As a result, pipeline companies bid up the price of natural gas, agreeing to extremely expensive take-or-pay contracts with producers. When crude oil prices eventually plummeted in 1982, natural gas prices soon followed, and many of these pipeline companies were eventually forced to renegotiate their contracts with producers or face bankruptcy, or both.

For decades, pipelines were wholesalers of natural gas to retail utilities or to large commercial and industrial companies. Their rates were subject to cost-based regulation by the Federal Power Commission, which later became the Federal Energy Regulatory Commission (FERC). Shortly after the passage of the Natural Gas Policy Act of 1978, which began wellhead deregulation of natural gas, a surplus of natural gas developed. This surplus became even more acute when oil prices collapsed and industrial customers switched from natural gas to oil. The pressure on the pipelines became unbearable, and as a result they sought permission to cut their prices selectively to large price-sensitive industrial customers. By 1985 the FERC had moved to a regulatory approach that allowed pipelines to choose "open status"—that is, to allow customers to purchase their own natural gas and arrange separately for transport. With the commodity price plunging at the wellhead, pipeline customers were eager to arrange for the purchase of natural gas. During the next decade, the real price of gas fell by between 30 and 50 percent to commercial and industrial customers and by about 25 percent for residential customers (table 4-5).[12]

Residential deliveries of natural gas are handled by regulated monopolies—retail gas utilities—that in most cases are regulated by the same state commissions that regulate electricity and telephone services. These commissions could attempt to erect the cross-subsidies between commercial/industrial customers and residential customers that are found in telephony, but the ability of large industrial and commercial customers to

Table 4-5. *Real Price of Natural Gas in the United States, 1970–94*
1992 dollars per million Btu

Year	Residential	Commercial	Industrial
1970	3.46	2.45	1.24
1972	3.52	2.57	1.37
1974	3.69	2.73	1.74
1976	4.35	3.61	2.71
1978	4.95	4.32	3.26
1980	5.96	5.50	4.17
1982	7.19	6.70	5.41
1984	7.84	7.11	5.44
1986	7.03	6.13	3.97
1988	6.18	5.24	3.37
1990	6.01	5.02	3.15
1992	5.72	4.75	2.91
1994	5.93	5.10	2.96

Source: Energy Information Administration, *State Energy Price and Expenditure Report 1995* (Department of Energy, 1998), tables 6, 7, 8.

bypass these retail utilities surely places severe limits on such a strategy of cross-subsidization. As a result, residential rates are generally above commercial rates, and often much higher (table 4-4). Ironically, in regulating interstate sales of gas in the shortage era, the Federal Power Commission induced bypass into the intrastate jurisdiction by industrial and large commercial customers, thereby raising the relative prices to retail utilities and their residential customers. Note that the ratio of residential to commercial prices was highest in the most regulated period shown in table 4-4, namely, 1970–76.

Regression analysis of residential natural gas prices or the ratio of residential to commercial gas prices provides much the same result as the analysis described above for electricity. Rates are unrelated to the average population density in a state. The northeastern and southeastern regions of the country have significantly higher rates than the rest of the country, and high-income states have slightly higher rates. Otherwise, political and demographic variables have little influence on the level of residential rates per million Btus or the ratio of residential to commercial rates.

As with electricity, there is little evidence of a deliberate policy to cross-subsidize residential or rural consumers of natural gas from business or urban rates. The absence of a distinct inverse relationship between population density and residential gas prices could suggest a mild cross-subsidy, but these differences in density across entire states do not necessarily reflect differences in the average population density in consuming areas. We conclude that the state regulators who regulate electricity, natural gas, and telephone services follow very different approaches in terms of cross-subsidies and universal service. For some reason, telephone service is unique in the political demands it places on regulators for cross-subsidization.

Low-Income Energy Assistance

Although it does not qualify as a "universal service" policy as traditionally defined, the U.S. Low-Income Home Energy Assistance Program (LIHEAP) provides the states with more than $1 billion a year to subsidize low-income households' heating and cooling costs. The states, in turn, determine the eligibility standards for the program, with most setting an upper limit of 150 percent of the official U.S. poverty level or less. In 1995 approximately 5.5 million households received $1.5 billion in assistance from the LIHEAP program. The average benefit level was about $200 per household. Given that the average low-income household spent $326 per year on heating in 1995 and the average low-income household that incurred cooling expenses spent $109 for home cooling, the LIHEAP subsidies represented a significant share of these expenditures for households that availed themselves of the subsidy payments. However, less than 30 percent of eligible poor households received the subsidy in 1995.[13]

Like the rural electric subsidy program, the LIHEAP program is a direct subsidy program funded from general revenues. It does not involve concealed cross-subsidies that distort resource allocation in the sector delivering the service. Moreover, it is targeted to low-income consumers. The actual subsidies received by low-income households under this program, about $200 a year, are very large compared with the implicit subsidies received by these households for local telephone connections. Since less than 30 percent of eligible households avail themselves of this subsidy, however, the cost per low-income household is less than $60.00 a year. The efficiency losses of this program to the U.S. economy are therefore equal to $60.00 per eligible household (or $200 per participating household) times the efficiency costs of raising U.S. tax revenues, which are in the range of $0.26 to $0.40 per dollar raised.[14] Including the administrative costs of the program, the total efficiency losses to the U.S. economy of LIHEAP are thus in the range of $390 million to $600 million a year, a pittance compared with the welfare losses owing to the universal service policy in telephone.[15]

Regulated "Public Utilities": Is There a Consistent Pattern?

Perhaps the most surprising result in our analysis of state regulation of electricity, natural gas, and telephone service is how much they differ. When we examine the ratio of average residential to commercial rates across states, we find no significant correlation between the ratio for natural gas and the ratio for electricity.[16] And both ratios are inversely correlated with the ratio of residential to business flat rates for local telephone service, although this inverse correlation is once again not significant. One might have thought that traditionally Democratic states, such as Maryland or West Virginia, might attempt to erect cross-subsidies in all three utility sectors, while more conservative states, such as Utah, Wyoming, and New Hampshire, would not. In fact, there is no systematic pattern across the three sectors.

We have also found that in 1994, regulated residential rates for natural gas were about 16 percent more than those for commercial customers, and residential electricity rates were about 10 percent more than commercial electricity rates, undoubtedly because residential service is more costly per unit of energy than is commercial service. At the same time, the thirty-eight states that had flat rates for both residential and business telephone local service charged small- and medium-size businesses more than twice the residential rate for connections. Given that many of the same general political pressures must affect all three decisions from the same regulatory commission, we conclude that there must be strong historical reasons why telephone service has been singled out for a policy of cross-subsidization. It may be that competitive bypass explains the absence of cross-subsidies in natural gas, but we fail to see how most small- or medium-sized businesses could bypass a punitive universal service policy in electricity. Why are redistributionist regulators content to limit their attention to telephony?

Finally, regulation appears to add to the variance in prices. Residential electricity and residential natural gas rates should exhibit less variance across states than the basic energy commodity prices for oil, coal, and natural gas. The latter are likely to vary greatly across states because of

Table 4-6. *Variation in Rates across Forty-Eight States, 1994*
Coefficient of variation

Commodity or service	Coefficient of variation
Oil	0.082
Coal	0.310
Average residential rate for natural gas	0.199
Average residential rate for electricity	0.254
Large-city local residential telephone rate	0.338
Small-town local residential telephone rate	0.304

Sources: Authors' calculations based on Energy Information Administration, *State Energy Price and Expenditure Report 1995* (Department of Energy, 1998), and National Association of Regulatory Utility Commissioners, *Bell Operating Companies Exchange Service Telephone Rates* (Washington, 1994).

transportation costs from producing areas. However, the retail prices of electricity and natural gas should be less variable because electricity generation and retail distribution costs should be relatively similar across states after adjusting for population density. In fact, the regulated residential energy rates exhibit greater variation across the states than does the price of oil, and only slightly less than does the price of coal (table 4-6). It is hardly surprising that urban and rural telephone rates exhibit the greatest variance of all even when standardized for large-city and small-town relative densities.

Cable Television

Cable television is surely not an essential "utility" service, but it would be difficult to identify any consumer service in the United States that is as ubiquitous and important to Americans as television. Television ownership is more pervasive than telephone service among U.S. households. Fully 98 percent of all households have at least one television set; most have two or more. Telephone service is subscribed to by 94 percent of households. About 70 percent of all U.S. households now receive their television service from a multichannel distribution service—cable television, satellite master antenna service (SMATV), multichannel multipoint (microwave) distribution service (MMDS), or direct broadcast satellites (DBS).

U.S. households subscribe to cable and other multichannel video services at fees that now average $30 to $35 a month because they prefer the vast selection from these services to off-air broadcasting choices. Most cable subscribers now receive more than fifty channels of services, and DBS subscribers have access to as many as 200 channels. Despite the key role of television, and the incredible enhancement of television service offered by the multichannel subscription services, there is no discernible "universal service" policy in place at the state or federal levels of government. No group of subscribers is subsidized so that its monthly charges remain "affordable." The average cable television bill rises very slowly with income. Although the industry has been subject to considerable regulation over its forty-year history, it has never been subjected to the rate distortions faced by the telephone industry.

Regulation

The regulation of cable began as a policy to protect off-air television broadcasting and was thus inherently anticonsumer and exceedingly costly in terms of the loss of economic welfare. In the 1960s and 1970s, cable systems were limited by the Federal Communications Commission's (FCC's) regulation of the services that they could offer.[17] Only a few distant broadcast signals could be imported into each market depending on the number of signals available off the air. "Pay" cable, such as the current HBO, Showtime, or Disney channels, was essentially blocked by FCC rules limiting the availability of filmed/taped programming over any form of pay television. These rules remained in place until the late 1970s when a series of court decisions and FCC rulings found them invalid or no longer necessary.

By the early 1980s, pressures began to mount to end the restrictive franchising of cable television by municipal authorities. For the first twenty years of cable's existence, cable television franchises had been awarded by municipal authorities, largely on a monopoly basis. The cities often extracted a large share of the resulting rents in the form of franchise fees, free municipal cable channels, or favors for politically influential local constituents. When the cities' right to limit cable-system competition began to be attacked in the courts, Congress began to consider legislation barring exclusive franchises and limiting municipal fees. In 1984 the Cable Communications Policy Act was passed, which eliminated all state and local regulation of cable rates (effective in 1986) except in areas where cable has market power, limited franchise fees to 5 percent of basic revenues, and barred restrictive franchise agreements.

In 1986 virtually all cable rate regulation came to an end. As a result, cable operators began to search for new services, expand their channel capacity, and raise their rates. By 1989 rate increases had cumulated to a level of more than three times the average increases in the consumer price index over the same period, and Congress was induced to reconsider its 1984 decision to deregulate the industry.[18] After several years of debate, Congress finally passed the 1992 Cable Act, which included sweeping new provisions for rate regulation. The act became law when Congress voted to override President George Bush's veto—the only time his veto was not upheld in his four-year term.

The 1992 act provided for strict rate regulation of basic cable service and other programming tiers, except for pay cable or "à la carte" services (services offered on a channel-by-channel basis). It also included provisions limiting vertical integration into programming and the overall share of the nation's cable systems by large multiple system operators (MSOs). It did not, however, have any universal service, cross-subsidy provisions to aid low-income or rural subscribers. Many of the rate-regulation provisions of the 1992 act were reversed in the 1996 Telecommunications Act, but most of the other provisions were retained.

Universal Service?

In the absence of any federal or state policies mandating "affordable" cable rates to poor or poorly located subscribers, it is likely that rates paid by subscribers reflect the cost of service. Therefore, one would expect cable-system rates to rise with declining population density but not to vary with household income. Two major sources of data largely confirm these expectations.

In 1993 the Federal Communications Commission collected data from a large sample of the nation's cable systems for the purpose of implementing provisions of the 1992 Cable Act. Detailed cable-system information was collected for 1986 and 1992. We use the 1992 data to determine the effects of various influences on basic cable rates. We wish to determine whether rates reflect differences in costs that are caused by system size, population density, and channel capacity. Rural subscribers live in areas that require more distribution plant per home passed; hence, we expect rates to vary directly with the miles of plant per home. Furthermore, there are some economies of scale in operating a system that should be

Table 4-7. *Sample Characteristics for Federal Communications Commission 1992 Cable Data*[a]

Variable	Mean	Standard deviation
Basic rate (*P*)	15.29	5.15
Miles per household (*M/HH*)	0.00377	0.132
Subscribers (*SUBS*)	3,927	13,795
Channels (*CH*)	19.6	10.4
Competition (*COMP*)	0.25	0.43
Public system (*PUBLIC*)	0.0021	0.14
Percentage underground (*UND*)	22.0	26.0
Buried subscriber drop lines (*BUR*)	0.13	0.34

Source: Federal Communications Commission cable television database as authorized in FCC, "Report and Order and Further Notice of Proposed Rulemaking in the Matter of MM Docket 92-266," FCC 93-177 (May 3, 1993), appendix E.

a. 387 systems.

reflected in system size. Finally, costs rise with the number of channels of service offered.

For the 484 systems in the FCC sample with complete data, we estimate

$$(4\text{-}1) \quad P = f(M/HH, SUBS, CH, COMP, PUBLIC, UND, BUR),$$

where *P* is the basic monthly rate, *M/HH* is miles of plant per household passed, *SUBS* is the number of subscribers to the system, and *CH* is the number of channels in the basic package. *COMP* and *PUBLIC* are dummy variables indicating the presence of a competitive cable system or a government-owned system passing 50 percent of the homes in the area. These latter variables are intended to capture the effects of competition on cable rates. We also include two other cost drivers: the proportion of cable plant that is underground (*UND*) and a dummy variable equal to one if a cable system must bury its subscriber drop lines but equal to zero if no such local requirement exists (*BUR*).

The means and standard deviations of all variables are shown in table 4-7. The results from estimating equation 4-1 in linear and log-linear form are shown in table 4-8. Clearly, the number of channels *(CH)* and the

Table 4-8. *Determinants of Basic Cable Rates, 1992*[a]

Variable	Linear model	Linear model	Log-linear model	Log-linear model
Constant	12.30	12.58	1.94	1.93
Miles per household (*M/HH*)	1.46	1.79	0.00096	0.104
	(0.86)	(1.04)	(0.23)	(2.83)
Channels (*CH*)	0.219	0.195	0.474	0.439
	(9.68)	(8.81)	(8.65)	(7.91)
Subscribers (*SUBS*)	-0.0000064	...	-0.0074	...
	(-3.79)		(-4.18)	
Competition (*COMP*)	-3.47	-3.54	-0.241	-0.265
	(-6.55)	(-6.71)	(-4.00)	(-4.31)
Public system (*PUBLIC*)	-4.47	-4.12	-0.230	-0.246
	(-1.58)	(-2.58)	(-1.35)	(-1.40)
Proportion underground (*UND*)	-0.0020	-0.0020	-0.0054	-0.0055
	(-2.124)	(-2.20)	(-2.31)	(-2.33)
Buried drop lines (*BUR*)	1.74	1.88	0.183	0.213
	(2.47)	(2.62)	(2.37)	(2.70)
R^2	0.284	0.259	0.269	0.232
Number of observations	387	387	328	328

Source: Authors' calculations based on FCC cable television database (see table 4-7).
a. *t* statistics in parentheses.

system size (*SUBS*) have significant effects on cable rates. Each additional channel increases the basic rate by twenty-two cents a month in the linear model; the elasticity of the rate with respect to basic channels is 0.47 in the log-linear model. Each addition of one thousand subscribers reduces the basic rate by less than one cent a month in the linear model.

The elasticity of the rate with respect to basic subscribers is −0.007 in the log-linear model. In addition, competition and government ownership of systems reduce the monthly rate by about 24 percent in this specification.[19] For our purposes, the most surprising result is that the basic rate does not vary with population density (miles/household passed). To some extent, this is the result of a strong direct correlation between system size and population density. When the number of subscribers is dropped from the equation, the statistical significance of miles per home passed (*M/HH*) rises.

In addition, the average number of basic channels is a direct function of the size of the cable system. Smaller, rural systems have much lower channel capacity on average than do the large-city systems. The average number of channels on FCC-sample systems with 5,000 or more subscribers was twenty-seven, but only nineteen for systems with fewer than 5,000 subscribers. Therefore, rural subscribers had a much lower-quality service than their urban brethren, even as recently as 1992. In turn, they paid about twenty cents less a month for each reduction in channel capacity, but Robert Crandall and Harold Furchtgott-Roth found that each additional basic satellite or broadcast signal available to subscribers was worth at least seventy cents a month in the early 1990s.[20]

A more recent source of cable rate data is the bill-harvesting database assembled by PNR and Associates for telephone rates. Approximately 60 percent of the households sampled by PNR in 1995 had cable service. These households reported their total month's cable bill, not the basic cable charge. As seen in table 4-9, the average cable expenditure across 6,006 households was $31.92 a month. The distribution of cable bills across households by income and size of metropolitan statistical area (MSA) reveals very little variance. In general, expenditures rise with income, but at a very slow rate. The lowest-income households spent $30 a month; the highest-income households spent about $35 a month. Similarly, rural (non–metropolitan statistical area) households spent $29 a month, while those in the largest MSAs spent about $35.50 a month. These differences could reflect differences in basic cable rates, but they are more likely to reflect the tendency of large-market, high-income households to purchase

Table 4-9. *Average Household Expenditures on Cable Service, 1995*
Dollars, except as indicated

Annual income	Average cable bill	Population of MSA (thousands)	Average cable bill
All households	31.92	All	31.92
Less than 10,000	30.32	Non-MSA (rural)	28.98
10,000–19,999	29.94	50–250	30.70
20,000–39,999	31.44	250–500	30.77
40,000–74,999	33.03	500–1,000	31.02
75,000 or more	34.93	1,000–2,500	32.94
		2,500 and over	35.58

Source: PNR and Associates, *Bill Harvesting II* (Jenkintown, Pa., 1995).

more discretionary cable services, such as pay cable or other higher tiers of service. Moreover, given that rural systems have decidedly fewer channels of service than large, major-city systems, the difference between average rural and large-MSA cable bills is surely less than the difference in the average value of service between them.

When we use the PNR data to estimate the effect of household size, income, and population density on monthly cable expenditures, the household and household income variables have highly significant, positive coefficients, but population density has a small and only marginally significant positive effect. Thus it appears that rural subscribers spend slightly less on cable service, but much of the difference may reflect differences in household incomes. Once again, given the differences in channel capacity across areas of different population density, we conclude that rural households pay more for a given quality of service than do their big-city brethren.

These results suggest that rural Americans pay slightly more for cable service because of the higher costs of physical plant per household in areas of lower population density and the lower channel capacity of rural systems. This could only occur in the absence of a universal service policy. Nevertheless, the differences in total cable spending by households in rural areas and those in large MSAs in the PNR bill-harvesting database are small and partly reflect differences in spending on higher tiers of cable service (table 4-9). Whatever the explanation, the differences in market-driven burdens on households across income levels and geographical areas are so small that one is left to wonder how universal service became such an issue in telephony.

Conclusion

A review of the regulated utility and nonutility services delivered to U.S. households through networks that share some of the characteristics of telephone networks leads us to conclude that federal and state regulation of these other services is neither driven by nor encumbered by "universal service" requirements. The only major exception is the long-standing federal program of subsidizing rural electric cooperatives through the Rural Electrification Administration (now the Rural Utilities Service), but even this program has been scaled back considerably. There is also a direct low-income subsidy program for home heating and cooling. However, only telephony is burdened by enormous cross-subsidies, paid by businesses, some urban residents, and heavy long-distance users, designed to keep rates for rural "high-cost" areas artificially low.

5 | Household Demand: Monthly Rates and "Universal Service"

Underlying the universal service policy of setting low monthly residential rates to induce households—regardless of their income or location—to subscribe to telephone service is the theory that low subscription rates achieve this purpose. Surprisingly, little in the existing literature suggests that such policies will achieve universality in telephone subscription.

The Literature

The literature on the demand for residential telephone connections is sparse and unsatisfying. Lacking data for individual households, most investigators attempt to relate average characteristics of geographic areas—such as states or provinces—to the level of telephone penetration in those areas. Unfortunately, in most of these studies, particularly those using Canadian or U.S. data, the investigators do not have a precise mapping of telephone rates into these geographic areas because rates vary across each state or province. In most U.S. states, local rates differ widely across cities or between cities and rural areas. For example, in 1996, a residential subscriber in Cadiz, Kentucky, would have paid only $14.67 a month for flat-rate service while a residence in Louisville would have paid $20.05.[1] Thus, any attempt to use a single average local rate for Kentucky would result in a substantial underestimate for Louisville residents and a substantial overestimate for Cadiz residents.

Nevertheless, the studies that have been published suggest a very low and declining price sensitivity of demand for local service.[2] The most comprehensive of the early studies was produced by Lewis J. Perl, who used individual household data from the 1970 census.[3] He found that the elasticity of demand for local residential service with respect to the monthly price was −0.04 and that the elasticity with respect to the connection charge was −0.02. However, Perl could not match each household with the precise rate it paid, and so he was forced to use a geographically averaged rate. Subsequently, Perl used the household data from the 1980 census and was able to match urban households with precise data on local rates. His logit model resulted in estimated price elasticities that were as low as −0.01 in areas with high penetration but were higher in areas of low income and thus lower penetration.[4] At a penetration rate of 88 percent and a flat monthly rate of $10 (approximately the average in 1983), Perl's results suggest a price elasticity of demand with respect to the monthly rate of −0.055.[5] In both studies, household income was a major determinant of the decision to subscribe to telephone service.

A survey of the other studies of the residential demand for telephone service are found in table 5-1. Real household incomes and telephone penetration have risen considerably since the last Perl study. It is not surprising, therefore, that the most recent studies, by Christopher Garbacz and Herbert Thompson Jr. and by Ross Eriksson, David Kaserman, and John Mayo, find that the price elasticity of demand for local residential service is much lower—between −0.026 and −0.01.[6] However, Garbacz and Thompson find that the elasticity with respect to the one-time connection charge is about double this level. Based on these results, one might make a mild case for subsidizing one-time connection charges, but the case for widespread suppression of all continuing monthly residential rates through internal cross subsidies is surely much weaker.

Some Evidence from International Cross-Sections

In chapter 1, we provided some impressionistic evidence of the relationship between total telephone lines per person, telephone rates, and

Table 5-1. Price Elasticity of Residential Demand for Telephone Service

Study	Estimated elasticity with respect to monthly rate	Estimated elasticity with respect to initial connection charge	Country (type of data)
Waverman (1974)[a]	−0.12	...	Canada (time series)
Alleman (1977)[a]	−0.17	...	USA (cross-section of cities)
Perl (1978)[b]	−0.04	−0.02	USA (cross-section of households)
Perl (1983)[b]	−0.03	−0.01	USA (cross-section of households)
Bodnar and others (1988)	−0.009	...	Canada (cross-section of households)
Taylor and Kridel (1990)	−0.04	...	USA (cross-section of census tracts)
Hausman, Tardiff, and Belinfante (1993)	−0.005	−0.021	USA (pooled time series, cross-section)
Garbacz and Thompson (1997)	−0.026 to −0.001	−0.046 to −0.027	USA (cross-section of states)
Eriksson, Kaserman, and Mayo (1998)	−0.011 to −0.014	−0.011 to −0.015	USA (cross-section of states)

Sources: See note 6 in text.

a. As reported by Lester Taylor, *Telecommunications Demand: A Survey and Critique* (Ballinger, 1980).

b. At a 93 percent penetration rate with a $10 monthly access price.

GDP per capita across countries in the Organization for Economic Cooperation and Development (OECD). In this section, we utilize a larger sample of countries to estimate the relationship between telephone rates and telephone penetration. The International Telecommunication Union compiles a variety of data for more than 200 countries, but reporting lags in the key series limit the usefulness of these data for recent years. As a result, we estimate the following relationship for 102 countries for 1990 and then for a more limited sample of 60 countries for 1995:

$$(5\text{-}1) \qquad LINES = f(P_{inst}, P_{loc\text{-}m}, P_{loc\text{-}c}, Y),$$

where *LINES* is the number of access lines per 100 persons, P_{inst} is the nonrecurring residential installation charge, $P_{loc\text{-}m}$ is the monthly residential charge for a local line, $P_{loc\text{-}c}$ is the price of a three-minute local call during prime calling hours, and Y is GDP per capita. All estimates are weighted by population to correct for heteroskedasticity. The results are shown in table 5-2 separately for high-income countries (per capita GDP of $6,000 or more) and lower-income countries (per capita GDP of less than $6,000).

The more interesting results for our purposes are those involving residential lines per 100 persons. Unfortunately, there are far fewer countries that report the residential share of total lines; hence, the results are less robust for the residential lines variable, particularly in 1995. We do not report results for developed countries in 1995, given that there are only thirteen usable observations. Note, however, that the 1990 results demonstrate the importance of the residential installation charge in explaining the proliferation of residential lines. In developed countries, the elasticity of residential lines with respect to the connection charge at the point of means is −0.15; in the less developed countries, it is −0.43. Moreover, the income elasticity at the point of means is only 0.54 for the developed countries in 1990 but 1.25 for the less developed countries. In every case, the connection charge proves to add more to the explanation of telephone penetration than does the recurring monthly charge. Unfortunately, this connection charge was much higher in less developed countries than in the wealthier countries, contributing to their much lower telephone penetration.[7]

In our 1995 sample, the mean number of residential lines per 100 persons for less developed countries was only 6.9, while for the developed countries it was 31.7. The 1995 results are much less satisfactory. For

Table 5-2. *Determinants of Telephone Penetration across Countries, 1990 and 1995*[a]

Variable	High-income countries, 1990	Low-income countries, 1990	High-income countries, 1995	Low-income countries, 1995
Dependent variable: Main lines per 100 persons				
Constant	31.46	−0.850	28.29	3.13
	(11.61)	(−2.24)	(3.15)	(4.12)
P_{inst}	−0.039	−0.0047	0.0027	−0.0018
	(−28.47)	(−3.83)	(0.08)	(−1.05)
P_{loc-m}	−0.688	−0.0051	−0.834	−0.452
	(−4.69)	(−0.07)	(−3.07)	(−3.72)
P_{loc-c}	−108.1	9.83	74.60	−38.02
	(−8.56)	(2.26)	(2.17)	(−2.83)
Y	1.92	3.91	0.812	4.947
	(19.76)	(27.94)	(1.98)	(9.66)
R^2	1.00	0.941	0.996	0.862
N	29	73	20	40
Dependent variable: Residential lines per 100 persons				
Constant	23.38	−1.47	. . .	2.01
	(7.00)	(−2.20)		(1.19)
P_{inst}	−0.024	−0.0037	. . .	−0.002
	(−9.29)	(−2.76)		(−0.53)
P_{loc-m}	−0.496	0.024	. . .	−0.38
	(−1.93)	(0.16)		(−1.49)
P_{loc-c}	−1.79	9.21	. . .	−18.05
	(−0.09)	(2.20)		(−0.81)
Y	0.971	2.97	. . .	3.78
	(8.81)	(17.89)		(6.67)
R^2	1.00	0.913	. . .	0.737
N	26	59	. . .	31

Source: Authors' calculations.
a. *t* statistics in parentheses.

residential lines, there is no systematic effect of any of the price variables, but income retains its significant influence—though at an elasticity at the point of means that is now only 0.9. For total lines per 100 persons, there now appears to be a statistically significant negative effect of the monthly residential charge and the local usage charge, but no such effect from the residential installation charge. These results may simply reflect the fact that residential rates have been reduced substantially by these developing countries and that those with the highest combined business and residential penetration have been able to reduce rates the most.

New Demand Estimates for the United States

The existing literature provides evidence that the demand for telephone service is extremely insensitive to the monthly charge for service and that the estimated price sensitivity is declining over time. It would be useful to corroborate this trend through an econometric analysis of more recent data, particularly from individual households. Unfortunately, we are unable to locate a source of such microdata that includes a large number of nonsubscribers whose precise location can be established. Instead, we are forced to rely on grouped data for the United States.[8]

To supplement this literature and to provide more current estimates, therefore, we rely on grouped data from the 1990 Census of Population and from the 1995 Current Population Survey (CPS). Neither provides us with much support for the theory that local monthly rates are important in determining residential telephone service subscription.

Current Population Survey

The most recent data on residential telephone subscriptions are obtained by the Current Population Survey. In three of its monthly surveys, the CPS canvasses its 55,000-household sample to determine whether the household has telephone service or at least has access to a telephone, say, through a pay telephone in its apartment complex. We are interested primarily in whether the household has telephone service in its own residence.

As we have seen, telephone service has become almost ubiquitous for all U.S. households with incomes above $20,000 a year; fewer than 4 percent of these households are without telephone service. Even among households with incomes below $10,000, however, telephone penetration is above 86 percent, but is this penetration the result of policies that keep monthly subscription rates low? Estimating a simple model of local telephone penetration, using CPS data, provides glimpses of an answer.[9]

We expect the demand for telephone service to be related to income, household demographics, the cost of installation, the household's location, the monthly price of service, and the existence of state subsidy programs

(Lifeline or Link-Up) to help pay for installation or monthly service. The CPS data are available for each state; therefore, we estimate for the forty-eight continental states models of the following form:

$$(5\text{-}2) \qquad\qquad PEN_i = X_i + u_i$$

$$(5\text{-}3) \qquad\qquad \text{Log } PEN_i = X_i + u_i$$

$$(5\text{-}4) \qquad\qquad \text{Log } [PEN_i / (1 - PEN_i)] = X_i + u_i,$$

where PEN_i is the proportion of households with a telephone in the ith state and the X_i are a set of independent variables that are likely to influence household demand for telephone service. These variables include per capita income (Y), the proportion of individuals under the official poverty level (POV),[10] the proportion of households with a black head (BL), the proportion of households with an Hispanic head $(HISP)$,[11] the installation charge for connecting a household (P_{inst}), the monthly charge for local service in the most dense and least dense areas served by the state's Bell operating company $(P_{m\text{-}urb}$ and $P_{m\text{-}rur})$, the proportion of the population living in rural areas (RUR), a dummy variable for the cold northern-tier states $(NORTH)$, and two dummy variables reflecting the existence of Lifeline and Link-Up subsidy programs $(LIFELINE^*POV$ and $LINKUP^*POV)$, scaled to reflect the eligible populations in poverty. Since all states now have Link-Up programs, we define $LINKUP$ as the number of years that the program has been in existence.

Because the left-hand variable in equations 5-2 through 5-4 is a measure of the proportion of households subscribing to telephone service drawn from a small sample of the entire universe of households in the state, the residuals may exhibit heteroskedasticity, requiring that we estimate each equation using a weighted regression technique known as the minimum chi-square method.[12] However, our initial unweighted estimates show no evidence of such heteroskedasticity with respect to the number of households in the state, and we therefore report only the estimates based on a feasible generalized least squares correction for heteroskedasticity.

The results of estimating the household demand relationships from 1995 CPS data for forty-five states are shown in table 5-3.[13] The first three columns show the results for the entire population. The first column reflects the estimates of the linear model 5-2; the second has the results of the semilog model 5-3; and the third exhibits the results of the logit model

Table 5-3. *Determinants of Telephone Subscription, 1995 CPS Data*[a]

(Equation) Dependent variable:	(2) PEN	(3) LogPEN	(4) LogPEN/(1-PEN)	(2') PEN	(3') LogPEN	(4') LogPEN/(1-PEN)
Sample:	All households	All households	All households	Low income	Low income	Low income
Constant	1.00 (25.68)	0.0060 (0.14)	4.10 (5.67)	1.017 (25.77)	0.033 (0.70)	3.24 (9.62)
POV	−0.0018 (−1.42)	−0.0019 (−1.40)	−0.038 (−1.63)	...	...	...
Y	0.00051 (0.38)	0.00054 (0.38)	0.0028 (0.116)	...	...	...
BL	−0.071 (−1.84)	−0.078 (−1.88)	−0.87 (−1.21)	−0.147 (−2.00)	−0.176 (−1.97)	−1.174 (−2.11)
HISP	−0.097 (−2.09)	−0.108 (−2.16)	−1.03 (−1.20)	−0.209 (−4.19)	−0.245 (−4.09)	−1.80 (−4.62)
RUR	−0.037 (−1.94)	−0.040 (−1.97)	−0.579 (−1.65)	−0.108 (−4.89)	−0.128 (−4.85)	−0.910 (−4.84)

NORTH	0.012	0.013	0.200	0.037	0.044	0.306
	(1.95)	(1.97)	(1.70)	(3.21)	(3.20)	(3.12)
P_{inst}	−0.00064	−0.00066	−0.016	−0.0028	−0.0032	−0.026
	(−1.73)	(−1.67)	(−2.41)	(−3.27)	(−3.13)	(−4.08)
P_{m-rur}	0.0011	0.00012	0.016	−0.00086	−0.00098	−0.011
	(0.78)	(0.79)	(0.60)	(−0.28)	(−0.27)	(−0.41)
P_{m-urb}	−0.00082	−0.00095	0.00028	0.0013	0.0013	0.020
	(−0.56)	(−0.60)	(0.01)	(0.38)	(0.33)	(0.71)
LIFELINE*POV	−0.00069	−0.00075	−0.013	−0.017	−0.020	−0.174
	(−1.38)	(−1.38)	(−1.38)	(−1.17)	(−1.15)	(−1.37)
LINKUP*POV	0.000014	0.000015	0.00014	0.00040	0.00047	0.0030
	(1.13)	(1.16)	(0.61)	(2.73)	(2.73)	(2.53)
R^2	0.661	0.663	0.609	0.491	0.486	0.515

Source: Authors' calculations.

a. t statistics in parentheses.

5-4.The last three columns show the same regressions (with income and poverty excluded) only for households with incomes of less than $10,000 a year.[14] For each population group, the results are very similar across all three formulations of the demand model.

The results in table 5-3 provide confirmation of the effect of demographic forces on telephone subscription. The proportions of black and Hispanic households are inversely related to telephone penetration, but only the Hispanic variable is statistically significant at standard confidence levels in every equation. The proportion of population in rural areas and in northern states is very important in explaining telephone subscription levels, particularly for the low-income population. Surprisingly, income levels contribute little to the explanation of telephone subscription, and the coefficient on the poverty rate—while negative—is not statistically significant.

We are most interested in the effects of telephone rates on subscriptions, particularly for the low-income households who are most likely to choose not to subscribe. Of the price coefficients in table 5-3, only the coefficient for the installation charge is statistically significant. At the point of means of the sample, the elasticity of overall telephone penetration with respect to the installation fee is approximately −0.025. For the low-income population, the elasticity is much higher: in the range of −0.10 to −0.15. The local-rate coefficients are never statistically significant, perhaps because of the use of statewide Bell operating-company urban and rural rates that can only be rough approximations of the different rates faced by households in the sample. Thus we find that the first-time installation charge is much more important in explaining telephone subscriptions than are the local rates, a result consistent with the fact that the *LINKUP* variable is statistically significant (and positive) in the low-income regressions, whereas the *LIFELINE* variable is not.

The results from CPS data are likely to be imprecise because of the small sample sizes for each state. Nevertheless, our results from the 1995 CPS data suggest that the installation charge is more important in driving penetration than are the recurring monthly charges. Reducing the installation charge by 50 percent could have a substantial effect in enrolling the last 6 percent of U.S. households without phone service today.

Census Data

Because U.S. telephone rates vary so much across geographical jurisdictions, it is necessary to use much more narrow geographic units of observation than the states in estimating a demand equation. Ideally, one should either use data for a given town or city in which rates are uniform or even the individual household as the unit of observation. But using household data requires addressing the problem of censored data for households not having telephone service in an era in which 94 percent of all households now have a telephone. For instance, one could not use the PNR bill-harvesting data because these data include no households without a telephone. The decennial Census of Population is therefore one of the best sources of recent (1990) data, because it provides telephone-subscription information aggregated to the level of a census tract or a town or city, as well as a public-use sample of data for individual households. We use data for cities and towns because the 1 percent public-use sample does not permit us to identify the precise geographical location of the household. The data for cities, towns, or places does allow us to match household characteristics with rates for telephone service obtained from the local-exchange companies.

The 1990 census lists 2,765 cities, towns, or "census designated places." We submitted the list of these towns to large local exchange carrier (LEC) firms so that they could provide us with the information on local-exchange residential rates and installation charges for each. In this way we obtained 1,897 usable observations from which to estimate a demand model. In this model, we include the price for flat-rate residential service in the town, city, or place (P_{loc}), as well as the intrastate (intra-LATA) long-distance rate for the 31–40 mileage band (P_{ld}), as explanatory variables. Because very few middle- or upper-income households do not have a telephone, we use two alternative measures of P_{loc}: the regular household single-line rate and the Lifeline rate that is available only to qualifying low-income households. Once again, we interact the share of households classified as below the poverty threshold (POV) with the LIFELINE and LINKUP dummy variables to account for the fact that these programs only affect poor households.[15] Finally, we use population density (DENS) to capture the access externality that flows to a potential subscriber from the other subscribers in the local area. Summary statistics for these data are shown in table 5-4.

Once again, we estimate three functional forms of the demand model. At first, the results were disappointing for the logit model (5-1′), providing positive coefficients for the poverty variable. On closer examination, we discovered that the effect of poverty was negative when poverty rates were low, but this negative effect diminished and became positive at high rates

Table 5-4. *Summary Statistics for 1990 Census Data for Cities and Towns*[a]

Variable	Mean	Standard deviation
Telephone penetration (PEN)	0.955	0.041
Median income (Y)	32.7	13.1
Proportion in poverty (POV)	0.122	0.084
Population density ($DENS$)	1.300	1.200
Proportion of households with black head (BL)	0.101	0.152
Proportion of households with Hispanic head ($HISP$)	0.094	0.163
Monthly residential flat rate (P_{loc})	14.57	2.96
Monthly residential flat rate reflecting Lifeline program (P_{loc})	10.16	5.12
Connection charge (P_{inst})	40.45	8.47
Intrastate long-distance rate, 31–40 miles (P_{ld})	1.22	0.26
Dummy variable for Lifeline program ($LIFELINE$)	0.627	0.484
Dummy variable for Link-Up program ($LINKUP$)	0.987	0.112

Source: Authors' calculations.

a. 1,897 observations.

of poverty. Our only explanation for this effect is that a poor household assigns a lower value to a telephone if there are few other nearby households in its income stratum, but that the telephone becomes more valuable when there are a larger number of poor households with which to communicate. As a result, we use both the poverty (POV) variable and a squared poverty term ($POVSQ$) in all of the regressions.

Our 1990 census results, including the ($POVSQ$) term are reported in table 5-5. The three models yielded virtually identical results.[16] In every case, residential penetration is inversely and significantly influenced by the initial connection charge but not by the local monthly charge or the intrastate long-distance rate. All other coefficient estimates are of expected sign and are highly significant.

In every case, telephone penetration is inversely related to the poverty rate, but the effect of poverty diminishes as the share of households in poverty increases. The share of households with a black or Hispanic head is associated with much lower telephone penetration rates. The much more precise census data provide strong evidence that telephone subscription rises with median household income. Population density always has a

Table 5-5. *Demand for Telephone Service, from Grouped 1990 Census Data for Cities and Towns*[a]

Equation	Constant	P_{loc} [b]	P_{ld}	P_{inst}	LIFELINE*POV	LINKUP*POV	Y	POV	POVSQ	BL	HISP	DENS	R^2
Linear (1a)	1.003 (146.6)	0.00017 (0.94)	0.00096 (0.44)	−0.00070 (−9.51)	0.016 (1.30)	−0.098 (−5.06)	0.00048 (7.09)	−0.282 (−6.43)	0.292 (2.83)	−0.034 (−5.30)	−0.032 (−5.82)	0.0047 (5.22)	0.736
Linear (1b)	1.003 (153.5)	0.00016 (1.08)	0.0012 (0.59)	−0.00071 (−9.55)	0.022 (1.39)	−0.098 (−5.15)	0.00049 (7.17)	−0.285 (−6.44)	0.292 (2.81)	−0.034 (−5.27)	−0.032 (−5.95)	0.0047 (5.23)	0.736
SemiLog (2a)	0.024 (0.33)	0.00021 (1.05)	0.0012 (0.50)	−0.00075 (−9.21)	0.018 (1.29)	−0.109 (−5.38)	0.00051 (6.89)	−0.273 (−5.60)	0.231 (1.97)	−0.036 (−5.11)	−0.035 (−5.69)	0.0051 (5.19)	0.725
SemiLog (2b)	0.0030 (0.41)	0.00020 (1.21)	0.0016 (0.66)	−0.00076 (−9.30)	0.026 (1.42)	−0.110 (−5.49)	0.00051 (6.98)	−0.276 (−5.62)	0.230 (1.94)	−0.036 (−5.09)	−0.035 (−5.81)	0.0051 (5.20)	0.725
Logit (3a)	3.55 (15.85)	0.0028 (0.54)	0.118 (1.97)	−0.016 (−9.06)	−0.015 (0.06)	−1.235 (−2.17)	0.049 (17.27)	−12.15 (−7.81)	28.55 (8.13)	−1.161 (−8.74)	−1.231 (−10.29)	0.109 (6.34)	0.549
Logit (3b)	3.60 (17.16)	−0.00093 (−0.22)	0.125 (2.12)	−0.015 (−8.86)	−0.080 (−0.23)	−1.216 (−2.12)	0.049 (17.29)	−12.16 (−7.80)	28.61 (8.19)	−1.162 (−8.69)	−1.244 (−10.62)	0.109 (6.33)	0.549

Source: Authors' estimates.

a. *t* statistics in parentheses.

b. Regressions 1a, 2a, and 3a use the regular monthly flat rate for P_{loc}; regressions 1b, 2b, and 3b use the Lifeline rate for P_{loc}

significant and positive coefficient, a result consistent with the modern theory of telecommunications demand. The elasticity for the poverty rate is approximately -0.025 in most of the estimated equations. The elasticity for the share of households with a black or Hispanic head is approximately -0.003.

In each regression, telephone subscription is inversely related to the first-time connection charge. Since our dependent variable, *PEN*, has a mean value of 0.955 and a standard deviation of 0.041, it is not surprising that the estimated elasticities with respect to any of the relative price or demographic variables are extremely low. The elasticity of penetration with respect to the charge for connecting a new subscriber is between -0.025 and -0.030. And we are unable to find that the local monthly rate has any significant impact on the decision to subscribe to telephone service. The long-distance rate is significant only in the logit estimates, but its coefficient is positive. We have no explanation for this curious result.

Surprisingly, every estimate shows that telephone subscription is inversely related to the existence of a Link-Up program that reduces the connection rate. This result may simply reflect the fact that there were only two states in our sample—Delaware and Illinois—without a Link-Up program and that the state regulators in these states do not feel compelled to participate in the federal program because telephone subscription among low-income households in their states is already relatively high. Put another way, the results on *LINKUP* could just as easily reflect causation that runs from penetration to the decision to adopt the program as from the opposite direction.[17] The Lifeline program has no statistically significant effect on telephone subscription—either through the coefficient of the *LIFELINE* variable or of the P_{loc} variable when it is adjusted to reflect the discount for the Lifeline program.

New Results for Canada

Further useful evidence on the determinants of household demand for telephone service may be obtained from recent Canadian data. It is possible to use the Canadian Family Expenditure Survey to obtain data on household subscription to the telephone network and to combine these data with published telephone tariffs across provinces.[18] We asked Statistics Canada to insert the relevant telephone rates for each of 9,492 observations drawn from the 1992 Family Expenditure Survey and to estimate a logit

Table 5-6. *Mean Values for Income and Price Variables, Canada, 1992*
Canadian dollars

Variable	Mean
Household income (thousands of dollars) (Y)	46.1
Long-distance rate, 5 minutes, daytime (P_{ld})	1.58
Local monthly rate (P_{loc})	10.55
Connection charge (P_{inst})	25.50

Source: Statistics Canada, *Family Expenditure in Canada, 1992.*

model (equation 5-4) of household telephone subscription. The regression model included as independent variables the same three rate variables as in our U.S. regressions above, as well as family income (Y), household size (N), and two dummy variables indicating whether the household received Social Assistance ($ASST$) and whether the head of household was not a citizen of Canada (ALI). Mean values of the relevant data are shown in table 5-6; the results are shown in table 5-7.

The most puzzling result is the coefficient on the installation rate, which is positive in both specifications.[19] The elasticity of subscription for the long-distance rate is consistently negative, and the elasticity for the monthly local rate is negative when the equation is estimated without the family-size variable. The coefficients for family income and social assistance have the expected signs, and the coefficient of the non-Canadian citizen variable—like the coefficient on Hispanic head of household in the U.S. equations—is also negative.

The elasticities that emerge from the estimates in table 5-7 are extremely low. The income elasticity of telephone penetration at the point of means is just 0.022, while the price elasticities are −0.00048 for the long-distance rate and −0.0003 for the local monthly rate. Once again, these estimated elasticities provide little support for using below-cost, recurring monthly rates as a policy tool for promoting universal service.

Implications for Universal Service Policy

Our demand estimates for the United States are roughly consistent with those of Christopher Garbacz and Herbert G. Thompson and of Ross C. Eriksson, David L. Kaserman, and John A. Mayo.[20] They lead to the inevitable conclusion that attempting to promote universal service by

Table 5-7. *Logit Estimates of Canadian Household Demand for Telephone Subscription, 1992*[a]

Variable	(1)	(2)
Constant	3.40	3.80
P_{inst}	0.007	0.006
	(0.0005)	(0.0005)
P_{loc}	0.0005	−0.01
	(0.0007)	(0.00075)
P_{ld}	−0.166	−0.102
	(0.01)	(0.01)
Y	0.0092	0.016
	(0.000094)	(0.000088)
N	0.256	. . .
	(0.002)	
$ASST$	−1.177	−1.03
	(0.0045)	(0.004)
ALI	−0.572	−0.628
	(0.008)	(0.006)

Source: Estimates by Statistics Canada, as requested by authors.
a. Standard errors in parentheses.

cross-subsidizing local service through higher long-distance rates is not only expensive but also not very effective. The sensitivity of telephone penetration to the recurring monthly price is so small that it is increasingly difficult to detect in modern studies.

Our results provide only modest support for the current Lifeline policy that generally targets low-income households. We find—except for the Canadian demand estimates—that telephone subscription is sensitive to the first-time connection charge, but curiously, our 1990 U.S. Census results find that telephone penetration is inversely related to the current Link-Up program. Therefore, we would be hesitant to recommend that regulators subsidize even the installation charge to expand universal service. We are certain, however, that reducing the recurring monthly charge will not prove very fruitful in expanding telephone subscribership.

6 Costs and Benefits of Traditional Universal Service Policies

We are now in a position to provide an estimate of the costs and benefits of the traditional universal service policies that we detailed in the first chapter. In so doing, we focus solely on the United States, drawing on the evidence developed in earlier chapters on the patterns of household spending for telephone service in the United States, the extent of residential-telephone penetration, and the demand elasticities for local connections and long-distance services. We also delve into the various proposals to change universal service policy in the wake of the 1996 Telecommunications Act—transferrable "high-cost support"—and the cost models that have recently been developed to implement these changes and to guide the post-1996 interconnection policy. We do not, however, attempt to derive similar estimates of the cost of the universal service policies in other countries because we simply lack the data on costs, the distribution of expenditures and usage patterns across geographical areas, and telephone rates.

The Universal Service Goals

As we have seen, universal service has been a political concept, one often defined to justify changing telecommunications policies in the

United States. In this chapter, we ignore the Theodore Vail rationale for keeping AT&T's monopoly intact because we see little to be gained from estimating the effects of what certainly would be a misguided policy today, and one that may have been misguided at its birth.

We assume that modern and postmodern universal service policies are mechanisms designed for one or more of three purposes:

—To ensure that everyone has access to a telephone;

—To redistribute income from rich to poor and from urban to rural telephone subscribers;

—To capture the externalities from telecommunications in certain service sectors, such as education, health care, and libraries.

In this chapter we provide quantitative estimates of the benefits and costs of the current pursuit of the first two of these goals.

Universality of Basic Residential Telephony

As we showed in chapter 1, almost everyone in wealthy societies now has a telephone in his or her residence. And the evidence on demand elasticities suggests that the principal instrument in universal service policies—keeping local access and usage charges low—is unlikely to have a major effect on subscriptions to the network. As a result, the benefits of such policies in terms of increasing penetration cannot possibly be very great. Given our econometric results, we estimate that even a doubling of local flat rates (or "line rentals") would reduce primary residential subscriptions—the first line into the residence—by only about 0.3 percent.

How much higher would local residential rates be in the absence of a universal service policy? Obviously, the answer to this question depends on assumptions about cost functions and the institutional climate that would exist in the absence of these policies. If regulation were to continue anyway, local residential rates might gravitate to the average historical ("embedded") cost of local service. For the United States, this might be as much as $40 per access line, or approximately double the average flat rate for residential service today. If we were to assume that rates could be set at estimated forward-looking incremental costs, rates might remain in the $20 range on average, rising in rural areas and falling in urban areas.[1]

Finally, if total deregulation of rates were to occur, local rates might rise substantially until constrained by new entrants or subscribers' switching to wireless services. Given wireless personal communication service

(PCS) rates that are now about $0.10 a minute in markets with three or four wireless carriers, local rates could rise to as much as $100 a month if the incumbent local exchange carriers (ILECs) decided to pursue a short-term strategy, but fall thereafter.[2]

Contesting Cost Models

To estimate the effects of universal service policies, we begin by analyzing the effect on subscriber penetration of allowing rates to rise to various measures of costs. To estimate these costs, we begin by drawing on the two contending models—Hatfield 5.0 (advocated by the large U.S. long-distance companies) and Benchmark Cost Proxy Model 3.1 (BCPM 3.1) (advanced by the U.S. ILECs)—that have appeared in regulatory proceedings as the result of the Telecommunications Act—as well as the Federal Communications Commission's own Hybrid Cost Proxy Model (HCPM). These models, designed to estimate forward-looking long-run incremental costs, provide very different estimates in large part because of different assumptions about the cost of capital, the optimal design of the local company's plant, and various assumptions about overhead expenses. To gain some understanding of this difference, look at the models' estimates of the forward-looking cost of a residential line in two states, one urban state (California) and one rural state (Mississippi) in table 6-1.[3] Note the very large differences between the Hatfield and BCPM estimates. The weighted average of the cost per residential lines across all U.S. regional Bell operating companies (RBOCs) plus SNET is $18.31 a month for the Hatfield model and $33.89 for the BCPM. Given average residential rates in the vicinity of $20.00 a month, the Hatfield model suggests no general revenue deficiency of local residential flat rate service while the BCPM would suggest a deficiency of about $18 billion a year.

Much of the difference between the models derives from their assumptions about the cost of capital, depreciation rates, and facilities sharing (with other utilities). The FCC at one time attempted to narrow this difference by specifying a "common" list of inputs for each model. Indeed, when these input values are substituted in the models, the differences narrow substantially. We therefore show this compromise between the two contesting models as Common-Input model, "CI," in table 6-1. Because the FCC uses regulatory accounting assumptions concerning depreciation and the cost of capital, the common-input estimates generally tend to settle somewhat closer to the Hatfield model than to the BCPM base-case

Table 6-1. *Four Estimates of the Forward-Looking Incremental Cost of Local Residential Service*

Dollars/month

State	Cost model	0–5 lines/ sq. mi.	5–100 lines/ sq. mi.	100–200 lines/ sq. mi.	200–650 lines/ sq. mi.	650–850 lines/ sq. mi.	850–2,550 lines/ sq. mi.	2,550–5,000 lines/ sq. mi.	5,000–10,000 lines/ sq. mi.	10,000+ lines/ sq. mi.
CA	Hatfield	105.76	37.84	23.79	18.22	15.91	14.58	13.11	11.88	9.61
CA	BCPM[a]	167.03	65.60	38.57	32.47	30.48	27.55	26.09	22.89	20.03
CA	CI[b]	129.88	45.12	29.64	25.86	24.41	22.66	21.59	20.07	18.14
CA	HCPM[c]	275.36	65.11	32.51	24.33	22.17	19.02	17.37	14.24	11.87
MS	Hatfield	117.05	53.99	25.87	20.50	18.36	15.81	13.32	11.75	8.99
MS	BCPM[a]	162.55	77.39	40.36	35.13	32.62	30.18	27.76	23.89	20.82
MS	CI[b]	117.61	52.22	31.05	27.97	25.42	24.17	22.22	20.57	19.08
MS	HCPM[c]	221.68	88.34	33.09	25.76	22.71	20.21	16.44	14.21	11.89

Source: Authors' estimates.

a. Benchmark Cost Proxy Model.

b. Common Input Model.

c. Hybrid Cost Proxy Model.

estimates. However, the common-input estimates are somewhat closer to the BCPM base-case estimates in the areas of greater line density but much closer to Hatfield base-case estimates in more rural areas.

Finally, we use the FCC's own HCPM that has been under development for three years as a guide to the commission's new explicit high-cost universal policy. This model reflects the commission staff's attempt to model the cost of standard voice-data service based on detailed mappings of subscriber location, perhaps the most detailed modeling effort undertaken thus far.[4] It generates a much steeper rate of increase in per subscriber costs with declining density than do the other three models.[5]

In the analysis that follows, we estimate the cost of current universal service policies using only the common-input (CI), the BCPM, and the HCPM models.[6] We do not use the Hatfield model in most of our work because the Hatfield model would require local-rate reductions. If the Hatfield model is correct, regulation has succeeded in keeping all U.S. telecommunications rates above cost, and optimization would surely require a fundamental shift away from regulation. Our objective in this analysis, however, is to estimate the effects of the relative distortions in prices occasioned by universal service policies in a regulated environment, not the extent to which regulation has reduced incentives for productive efficiency.[7]

Repricing Telephone Service

It is our intention to estimate the cost of universal service policies by providing a state-by-state estimate of the effects of moving to a "cost-based" pricing regime in 1996—one in which local rates are set at incremental costs based on the three models' estimation of them. While we do not believe that a market would adjust rates immediately to these forward-looking costs, we assume that rates would tend to approach these costs in long-run equilibrium.[8]

We divide each state into three regions—rural, suburban, and urban—on the basis of the March 1996 Current Population Survey (CPS), using the 1990 Census of Population to divide each state's households between urban and suburban for each MSA. Rural areas are areas outside MSAs. Suburban areas are areas within MSAs but outside the central cities, and urban areas are central cities in the relevant MSAs. For each of these regions in each state, we calculate the share of households in each of five income categories: less than $10,000; $10,000 to $19,999; $20,000 to $39,999; $40,000 to $74,999; and $75,000 and above.

Given the very low price elasticities of demand for local service that we and others have estimated from recent U.S. data, we use price elasticities of demand for local service that decline (in absolute value) from −0.0475 to −0.001 as we move from the lowest-income category to the highest.[9] Moreover, we assume that current telephone penetration rises from 0.88 in our lowest-income category to 0.92 in the highest-income category in the rural areas, and from 0.92 to 0.99 with rising income in MSAs.[10] We therefore estimate the number of primary residential subscribers from 1996 CPS data by applying these penetration rates in each of the density zones.

We distinguish between primary residential lines and second lines by using the HCPM model runs' estimates of second lines in each state, assuming that this ratio is constant across the state.[11] We use an estimated price elasticity of demand for secondary residential lines of −0.4, reflecting recent research.[12]

We also assume that the price elasticity of demand for long-distance service declines with income from −0.9875 to −0.575 across our five income categories.[13] We use the national average household expenditures on long distance for each region (rural, suburban, and urban) for each income category as our baseline—resulting in fifteen categories of average expenditure. Given the size of the PNR sample, we could not have disaggregated this baseline into separate estimates for each income group for each region in each state, or a total of 750 categories, because we would have been using averages based on fewer than 20 households in some instances.[14] However, we adjust each estimate for the effect of the long-distance rate in that state and geographical area by assuming a constant elasticity of demand at our assumed elasticities.[15]

The average local rates in existence in 1996 are based on data supplied by the Bell companies to the National Association of Regulatory Commissioners (NARUC). Where possible, rates were assigned to the density zones in table 6-1 based on subscriber-line counts by exchange size provided by the companies. Where these line counts were not available, we simply estimated the distribution from Census data on population within and without MSAs and the rates provided by the companies.[16] Although our estimates are for all residential subscribers in the state, we have data on rates only for the BOCs and SNET. We are therefore assuming that the rate structure, as well as the cost structure, for the BOC companies and non-BOC companies are the same for a given density zone in a given state. The average long-distance rates were calculated from PNR *Bill Harvesting* data for MSA and non-MSA households. The rates are a weighted average of intra-LATA and inter-LATA rates based on average minutes in each region for each class of service.

We assume that the repricing of residential service will result in local flat-rate increases that generate revenues to be applied to the reduction of intrastate long-distance rates and long-distance access charges in the state. For simplicity, we assume that all of these reductions are realized by residential subscribers. Business traffic accounts for about 60 percent of all long-distance activity; but business rates have already been competed down to a much lower level than residential rates.[17] In addition, a substantial share of business long-distance traffic is originated or terminated with "special access"—that is, private lines. As a result, it is difficult to know how much access rates for business traffic could be reduced. Moreover, estimating the consumer-welfare effects of lower business rates that are, in turn, passed through as lower consumer prices for financial, travel, entertainment, and other goods and services needlessly complicates our analysis.

Changes in Local Rates and Revenues

We begin by using the various cost models to estimate the revenue yield from repricing local flat rate service to estimated incremental cost. We cap the local rate at $100 a month, undoubtedly above the cap that would result from political influences, but a reflection of our view that any rate above $100 would quickly lead to the substitution of competitive wireless services for the LECs' wireline services. Given the small number of lines affected by this cap, it does not have an important effect on our calculations.

Rather than providing the reader with detailed estimates of the increase (or decrease) in the average flat residential rate for each state required if these rates are to be based on costs, we show the results for only four states, those listed in table 6-1 plus New Jersey and Wyoming, and for the entire United States. This allows us to exhibit our results for two urbanized states and two rural states as well as for the entire country.[18] These estimates, shown in table 6-2, reflect the very large differences among the four models (including the Hatfield model), with the Hatfield model often predicting average rate declines, especially in the more urbanized states, such as California. Note that even the Hatfield model finds that local

Table 6-2. *Average Effect of Cost-Based Repricing on Local Flat Residential Rates, 1996*

Dollars/month

State	Hatfield model	BCPM	CI model	HCPM
California	−4.36	9.44	4.40	1.20
New Jersey	0.07	11.03	6.87	4.26
Mississippi	10.33	27.70	14.31	25.87
Wyoming	3.08	20.66	11.32	18.31
United States	−0.76	13.62	6.65	5.03

Source: Authors' estimates based on HCPM geocoded subscriber line counts.

residential rates in rural states, such as Mississippi and Wyoming, are generally well below forward-looking incremental cost, thereby justifying at least some rate increases.

The Effect on Subscriber Penetration

Clearly, the estimated effect on subscriber penetration depends on the model chosen to estimate the cost-based local rates. In most states, the Hatfield model predicts lower average local rates and, as a consequence, higher residential penetration, particularly in urban and suburban locations. The BCPM, however, predicts a rise in the average local rate of almost two-thirds and, therefore, generally lower average subscriber penetration. As expected, the CI and HCPM models produce results between the other two. All four models predict much greater increases for rural flat rates than for urban rates. Thus, regardless of the model, repricing raises local rural rates relative to local urban rates.

The effect of cost-based local-rate rebalancing on subscriber penetration under each of the models on our four selected states is shown in table 6-3. Little subscriber-line loss occurs in all urban areas under even the BCPM, the model with the highest estimated forward-looking costs. Even in rural areas, primary subscriber-line loss is less than 5 percent and often much less. Only about one-third of that loss is among households with low incomes (less than $10,000 a year). In the most urbanized states, total residential line loss owing to cost-based rate rebalancing averages less than 1 percent, even when the BCPM is used. (Positive entries reflect situations in which rebalancing is estimated to require a rate decrease.) In rural states,

Table 6-3. *Effect of Cost-Based Repricing of Residential Service on the Number of Primary Residential Subscriber Lines*
Percentage change

Cost model	California	Mississippi	New Jersey	Wyoming
Central cities				
Hatfield	0.8	1.2	0.8	0.7
CI	−0.1	0.3	−0.2	−0.1
BCPM	−0.3	−0.1	−0.4	−0.5
HCPM	0.5	0.9	0.0	0.4
Suburbs				
Hatfield	0.3	0.7	−0.0	0.5
CI	−0.3	0.1	−0.6	−0.3
BCPM	−0.8	−0.4	−1.0	−0.8
HCPM	−0.1	0.4	0.0	0.1
Rural[a]				
Hatfield	−2.6	−1.4	. . .	−1.2
CI	−3.1	−1.7	. . .	−1.8
BCPM	−4.6	−3.1	. . .	−2.8
HCPM	−4.4	−2.9	. . .	−2.8

Source: Authors' calculations based on HCPM geocoded subscriber line counts.
a. No rural areas in New Jersey.

the loss averages about 3 percent. Overall, even using the highest-cost BCPM as the basis for rate rebalancing, the country loses less than 1.5 percent of primary residential access lines owing to cost-based rebalancing.

Long-Distance Rates

Full repricing results in some very large reductions in long-distance rates if the increased residential revenues are applied entirely to residential rates, often by more than current access charges. Yet, as table 6-4 shows, these reductions for our four highlighted states rarely bring long-distance rates down to less than six cents a minute, a level considerably above the rates, net of access charges, now being offered by major long-distance carriers.[19] If we were to apply the increased revenues to reducing all long-distance access charges—business and residential alike—the rate declines for residential subscribers would be more modest.[20] The largest reductions occur in the two rural states—Mississippi and Wyoming. This

Table 6-4. *Residential Long-Distance Rates Before and After Cost-Based Rate Rebalancing*

Dollars/minute

State[a]	Before rebalancing	CI model	BCPM	HCPM
Urban areas (MSAs)				
California	0.130	0.109	0.086	0.124
Mississippi	0.204	0.129	0.060	0.070
New Jersey	0.132	0.099	0.080	0.112
Wyoming	0.207	0.150	0.103	0.115
Rural areas				
California	0.120	0.100	0.076	0.115
Mississippi	0.180	0.106	0.037	0.046
New Jersey[b]	. . .	. . .	. . .	. . .
Wyoming	0.172	0.115	0.068	0.080

Source: PNR and Associates, *Bill Harvesting III* (Jenkintown, Pa., 1996); and authors' calculations.

a. All revenues derived from rebalancing are used to reduce residential long-distance rates.

b. No rural areas in New Jersey.

is no coincidence, given that these two states have the most distorted rates and the highest long-distance rates that are supporting these distorted local rates (table 6-2).

BCPM-based rate rebalancing still leaves long-distance in the range of five cents to ten cents a minute, far above the forward-looking cost of long-distance service. Obviously, the CI model leaves residential long-distance rates much higher—generally in the $0.10 to $0.13 per minute range. When the HCPM, with its relatively high estimates for the cost of serving residences in the most rural areas and its very low estimates of these costs in the most dense areas is used for rebalancing, long-distance rates are reduced by one-half to two-thirds in rural states but very little in the urbanized states (table 6-4). Indeed, California experiences virtually no reduction in long-distance rates at all because the HCPM estimates that local residential rates there are generally above cost.

The Welfare Gains from Repricing

The losses in economic welfare from abandoning the universal service policies that drive these distorted rates are clearly related to the relative changes in long-distance and local rates. Welfare losses from repricing toward cost occur because of the loss of subscriber lines, but the losses are more than offset by the gains that derive from increased long-distance telephone service. We assume that externalities generated by incremental subscribers are no more than $76.00 a year.[21] However, the gains from lower long-distance rates may be substantial, depending on the marginal cost of long-distance service. We assume that the forward-looking cost of long-distance service is $0.04 cents a minute. This is undoubtedly above the long-run incremental cost of providing long-distance service—assuming that originating and terminating access is priced at marginal cost.[22] However, for the sake of being conservative, we also show results based on a $0.06 marginal cost of long-distance service.

The resulting estimates of improvements in consumer welfare, excluding externalities, are shown in table 6-5.[23] Once again, we only show the results for the BCPM, CI, and HCPM models. There is very little repricing under the Hatfield model.

In every case, the net consumer welfare gain from repricing is positive—a result guaranteed by the fact that the demand for local connections is less price elastic than the demand for long distance. The distribution of these gains, however, is quite different across our four highlighted states. In California, with a small rural population, the low rural flat rates provide an enormous benefit to rural subscribers that cannot be recovered from the lower long-distance rates across the state. As a result, rural households—on average—gain substantially from the universal service pricing regime, that is, they incur large losses from cost-based rebalancing as exhibited in table 6-5. In Mississippi and Wyoming, however, a large share of households are in rural areas. Therefore, the policy of keeping local rates low in these states leads to very high long-distance rates—high inter-LATA access charges and high intra-LATA rates. Contrary to the result in California, rebalancing in these states often redounds to the benefit of even the average rural household.

The urban households in the rural states benefit far more than the urban residents of the urbanized states. To see this, we express the benefits of cost-based repricing on a per subscriber basis in table 6-6. While universal service policies may be popular in the rural states, they are exceedingly costly to many of these states' residents and may not even benefit the average rural household.

How are these gains distributed across income classes? In general, the higher-income classes gain the most per household (table 6-7)—these higher-income households make the most long-distance calls on average.

Table 6-5. *Monthly Consumer Welfare Gains from Cost-Based Repricing of Residential Telephone Service*
Millions of dollars

State	Central cities			Suburbs			Rural areas		
	BCPM	CI	HCPM	BCPM	CI	HCPM	BCPM	CI	HCPM
California									
From long distance	52.36	22.86	5.99	75.48	33.01	8.66	2.85	1.23	0.32
From local service	-32.33	-14.31	11.13	-71.10	-32.84	-15.31	-9.74	-6.06	-9.66
Net gain	20.03	8.55	17.12	4.38	0.17	-6.65	-6.89	-4.83	-9.34
Mississippi									
From long distance	1.98	0.92	1.82	2.38	1.10	2.19	28.45	12.97	26.13
From local service	-0.32	0.09	0.39	-0.41	0.06	0.37	-23.82	-12.92	-23.66
Net gain	1.66	1.01	2.21	1.97	1.16	2.56	4.63	0.05	2.47
New Jersey[a]									
From long distance	3.91	2.30	1.38	37.79	22.40	13.44	...	...	...
From local service	-1.18	-0.62	0.47	-34.09	-21.59	-14.31			
Net gain	2.73	1.68	1.85	3.70	0.81	-0.87			
Wyoming									
From long distance	0.84	0.43	0.73	0.29	0.15	0.26	3.48	1.74	3.01
From local service	-0.42	-0.15	-0.02	-0.16	-0.06	-0.02	-3.12	-1.83	-3.23
Net gain	0.42	0.28	0.71	0.13	0.09	0.24	0.36	-0.09	-0.22

Source: Authors' calculations.

a. No rural areas.

Table 6-6. *Monthly Benefits of Cost-Based Repricing of Residential Service per Basic Subscriber*
Dollars per subscriber

State	Central cities			Suburbs			Rural areas		
	BCPM	CI	HCPM	BCPM	CI	HCPM	BCPM	CI	HCPM
California	4.52	1.93	3.87	0.72	0.03	−1.10	−35.38	−24.73	−47.89
Mississippi	23.87	14.38	31.75	24.96	14.72	32.52	6.15	0.07	3.28
New Jersey[a]	9.14	5.66	6.22	1.49	0.33	−0.41	. . .	. . .	. . .
Wyoming	10.08	6.53	17.00	9.56	6.07	16.36	2.91	−0.70	−1.79

Source: Authors' estimates, using FCC's geocoded subscriber line counts.

a. No rural areas.

Table 6-7. *Distribution of Net Monthly Consumer Gains from Cost-Based Rebalancing, by Annual Income*
Dollars per subscriber

State	Cost model	Less than $10,000	$10,000–$19,999	$20,000–$39,999	$40,000–$74,999	$75,000 or more
California	BCPM	−1.97	−0.90	−0.08	3.31	5.56
California	CI	−1.25	−0.89	−0.44	1.12	2.25
California	HCPM	0.15	−0.43	−0.21	0.23	0.73
Mississippi	BCPM	−1.18	4.76	3.14	20.38	32.89
Mississippi	CI	−2.46	−0.21	−0.32	7.78	14.62
Mississippi	HCPM	−1.24	3.19	2.50	18.34	30.98
New Jersey	BCPM	−1.95	−0.34	0.02	4.04	5.31
New Jersey	CI	−1.61	−0.71	−0.48	1.90	2.74
New Jersey	HCPM	−0.71	−0.45	−0.42	0.85	1.28
Wyoming	BCPM	−3.68	1.17	0.19	10.96	19.42
Wyoming	CI	−3.17	−0.62	−0.95	4.53	9.20
Wyoming	HCPM	−3.83	0.63	−0.09	9.08	16.79

Source: Authors' calculations.

But recall our earlier discussion of calling patterns in chapter 3. Even among low-income subscribers, many make more calls than the average high-income household. Thus, the regressivity shown in table 6-7 ignores the fact that great gains are realized by some low-income households from cost-based rate rebalancing. In all four states, the average low-income subscriber loses from cost-based repricing, but these losses are very small. In states with large urban and small rural populations, such as Illinois, low-income households in rural areas lose substantially from cost-based repricing, and the gains to low-income households in urban areas do not offset these losses. In others, such as New York, low-income households in urban areas gain from rate rebalancing because their local rates decline. In such states, the universal service policy may redistribute income from urban to rural areas, but it does so even at the expense of the urban poor.

It is nevertheless surprising how little the lower-income households gain from the retention of universal service pricing policies and therefore lose from cost-based rate rebalancing In most cases, the lower-income households gain less than $2.00 a month from these universal service policies; in the most extreme case shown in table 6-7, the gain is but $3.83 a month.[24] However, the cost of these policies to higher-income Americans, who use their telephones more intensively, can be $15.00 to $30.00 a month, particularly in rural states.

The total welfare gains, including long-distance company gains, from this U-turn away from universal service pricing are significant. Under the BCPM, the gains are between $5.5 billion and $7.0 billion a year, depending on the assumed incremental cost of long-distance service (table 6-8). Under the CI model they are a somewhat more modest $3.4 billion to $4.1 billion a year, and using the HCPM, they are between $2.5 billion and $3.0 billion a year. In each case, the cost of universal service policy is very large for the amount of income redistribution or additional subscriber penetration generated.

With the BCPM, we find that households with incomes under $20,000 a year gain only $435 million a year from current (1996) universal service pricing policies. Furthermore, these universal service policies generate only 1.4 percent in additional subscribers. Middle- and upper-income U.S. telephone subscribers incur a net welfare loss of $4.1 billion, and producers (long-distance suppliers) sacrifice $1.9 billion to $3.4 billion to redistribute just $435 million to low-income households and to generate external benefits of only about $100 million a year. Surely, this is an expensive policy.

Table 6-8. *Annual Overall Effects of Universal Service Pricing Policies*
Millions of dollars

Cost model	Assumed marginal cost of long-distance service ($/minute)	Net welfare loss (excluding externalities)	Welfare gain to low-income households	Welfare loss to middle- and upper-income households	Producer surplus loss to long-distance suppliers	Externality value of increase in residential lines
BCPM	0.04	7,046	426	4,084	3,388	100
BCPM	0.06	5,479	426	4,084	1,822	100
CI	0.04	4,173	424	1,510	3,087	49
CI	0.06	3,404	424	1,510	2,318	49
HCPM	0.04	3,020	343	1,437	2,149	41
HCPM	0.06	2,489	343	1,437	1,570	41

Source: Authors' calculations.

Using the CI model, the net cost to middle- and upper-income house-holds is $1.5 billion and the cost to producers is $2.3 billion to $3.1 billion a year to generate $433 million in annual benefits for lower-income house-holds and only $49 million in external benefits from additional residential subscriptions. Finally, with the HCPM, we find that lower-income subscribers gain only $343 million a year from current universal service policies at an annual welfare cost of $1.3 billion to higher-income subscribers and a loss of $1.5 billion to $2.1 billion to producers. Regardless of the assumed cost model, this is a very costly income redistribution policy.

The Effect on Rural States and Rural Subscribers

Another goal of universal service policy is to ensure rural subscribers of low, "affordable" local telephone rates even though they generally live at the end of very long local loops that are expensive to build and to maintain. In general, rural subscribers enjoy local rates that are below urban rates. The degree to which rates are distorted is directly correlated with the share of rural households in a state. Put another way, the states that would enjoy the greatest benefits from cost-based repricing of service are the states with the largest share of rural subscribers. To show this, we report the estimated benefit per residential subscriber from repricing in the ten most and least urbanized states in our sample (table 6-9).

Clearly, the monthly cost to consumers of rate-distorting regulation is much greater in rural states than in urbanized states. States such as Maine, Vermont, Mississippi, and Montana have kept their local rural rates so low that a rebalancing of rates would benefit the average household by as much as $60.00 a year or more ($5.00 a month in table 6-9). Urbanized states like California, Arizona, Massachusetts, and New York, however, have reason-ably balanced rates and relatively few rural lines to support with revenues from other services; therefore, their residential subscribers would gain very little from further rebalancing, in some cases less than $5.00 a year. One obvious correlate of these distortions is the average long-distance rate paid by the state's residential subscribers. Rural states had long-distance rates in 1996 that were often in excess of $0.19 a minute, while the urbanized states had long-distance rates that were often below $0.15 a minute.

It is clear, therefore, that while rural states are the strongest supporters of universal service policies, these states' own residents pay a substantial price for these policies. Heavy users of long-distance services and urban residents

Table 6-9. *Average Monthly Consumer Gains from Rebalancing in the Ten Most Urban and Ten Most Rural States*
Dollars per subscriber

Most urban states	Net gain per subscriber			Average rural long-distance rate ($/minute)	Most rural states	Net gain per subscriber			Average rural long-distance rate ($/minute)
	BCPM	CI	HCPM			BCPM	CI	HCPM	
New Jersey	2.31	0.90	0.35	0.132[a]	Montana	7.59	2.10	2.49	0.165
California	1.64	0.36	0.11	0.120	Vermont	11.29	2.68	6.55	0.165
Massachusetts	0.47	0.02	0.18	0.128	Idaho	5.88	5.55	2.13	0.236
Connecticut	2.55	0.73	0.48	0.150[a]	Wyoming	5.14	1.55	4.10	0.172
Rhode Island	1.38	0.24	0.14	0.164[a]	Mississippi	9.16	2.46	8.04	0.180
Florida	2.88	0.91	0.40	0.177	South Dakota	5.18	1.80	1.31	0.211
Maryland	0.87	0.08	0.12	0.149	Maine	9.47	2.64	5.52	0.192
New York	0.30	0.09	0.45	0.139	North Dakota	4.61	1.78	0.80	0.191
Arizona	3.01	0.72	0.15	0.152	West Virginia	7.31	0.93	3.78	0.240
Nevada	3.75	1.53	2.43	0.196	Iowa	4.44	1.37	1.42	0.190

Source: PNR and Associates, *Bill Harvesting III*; and authors' calculations.
a. Average long-distance rate in urban areas; no data available for rural areas.

of these states are essentially taxed by regulators to keep the local rates low for rich and poor rural subscribers alike. Many of the urbanized states, however, impose a far smaller burden on residential users of long-distance services—not because they have necessarily rebalanced rates to cost, but because they have so few rural subscribers to support with revenues from other services. Table 6-10 shows the benefits from rebalancing rates for subscribers in rural areas. Rural subscribers, as a group, in every one of the most urbanized states benefit from existing universal service pricing policies and thus lose from cost-based rate rebalancing. The average rural subscriber in many rural states, however, may be worse off because of the current policies. Cost-based rebalancing would bestow benefits on rural residents in many rural states if the BCPM or CI cost models fairly characterize cost conditions. The HCPM, however, which produces cost estimates that rise much more rapidly with declining population density, suggests that rural subscribers would generally lose from rate rebalancing, even in the most rural states. It is crucial to recognize, however, that in the rural states, rural subscribers must tax themselves rather heavily (through higher long-distance rates) to keep their monthly rates low while in urbanized states there are many more city residents to pay the implicit tax.

Reducing Business Rates

All of our calculations thus far involve the rebalancing of residential local rates to some measure of forward-looking cost and using the resulting revenue gains to reduce long-distance rates dollar for dollar. Given that nonresidential (business) long-distance traffic is about 150 percent of residential traffic, efficient rebalancing of rates would require reductions in business rates as well. Business long-distance rates are already nearly 30 percent lower than residential rates, but even these rates would fall through cost-based reductions of access charges.[25] Moreover, the differences between business and residential rates (about five cents a minute in 1996 in the inter-LATA jurisdiction) could reflect differences in cost, perhaps in marketing costs. If all long-distance rates were to decline by the same absolute amount owing to rate rebalancing, business costs would decline, particularly in telecom-intensive sectors, such as hotels, retail and wholesale trade, finance and insurance, real estate, and restaurants. Most of these sectors are highly competitive; therefore, the reduced costs would quickly be reflected in their prices to consumers. Assuming that the derived de-

Table 6-10. *Monthly Effects of Cost-Based Rebalancing on the Average Rural Subscriber*

Dollars

Most urban states	Benefits to average rural subscriber			Most rural states	Benefits to average rural subscriber		
	BCPM	CI	HCPM		BCPM	CI	HCPM
New Jersey[a]	. . .	. . .	. . .	Montana	5.29	0.30	-1.91
California	-35.38	-24.73	-47.89	Vermont	4.71	-1.72	-1.57
Massachusetts	-16.86	-12.72	-21.61	Idaho	-2.14	0.59	-5.87
Connecticut	-23.31	-18.42	-26.89	Wyoming	2.91	-0.70	-1.79
Rhode Island	-13.24	-10.64	-18.00	Mississippi	6.15	0.07	3.28
Florida	-24.50	-15.94	-32.08	South Dakota	3.15	0.18	-1.24
Maryland	-27.36	-19.13	-35.04	Maine	4.43	-0.36	-0.04
New York	-34.42	-23.22	-39.40	North Dakota	3.28	0.39	-1.98
Arizona	-7.75	-5.52	-18.03	West Virginia	-4.98	-5.20	-9.15
Nevada	-20.22	-17.12	-40.21	Iowa	0.53	-1.73	-4.08

Source: Authors' estimates.

a. No rural areas.

mand for long-distance services in these sectors is more price elastic than is residential long-distance demand, there might be even greater gains available from cost-based repricing than those we have estimated.[26]

Once we allow for the fact that business long-distance rates fall alongside residential rates, however, the effects on income distribution change somewhat. An earlier study by one of the authors found that higher-income households spend about four times as much on the telecom-intensive services as do low-income households.[27] By contrast, high-income households spend only about 2.3 times as much as low-income households on long-distance service. Thus, if we have underestimated the welfare gains from abandoning the universal service pricing policy (for any given cost model), we have also underestimated the regressivity of such policy change somewhat.

Nor have we addressed the impact of moving local business rates to cost. This is a more difficult undertaking because many states—particularly the larger ones—have moved to usage sensitive business rates for smaller businesses.[28] Because we are lacking usage data, we could only guess at average business rates. In 1996 the average business single-line monthly rate was about $42 a month, or at least 20 percent above the average prediction of the cost per line from the BCPM. Were we to undertake a full rebalancing analysis, part of the additional revenues generated by moving residential rates to forward-looking incremental cost would surely have to be devoted to reducing local business rates in most states. Given that there is less than one business line for every two residential lines, the effect of lowering business rates to cost under the BCPM's assumptions would appear to divert about $4 per residential line from the reduction of long-distance rates to the lowering of local business rates. This would be a significant diversion in the urbanized states but would represent only about 20 percent of the increased local residential revenues in most rural states. Of course, in an analysis based on a model with lower forward-looking costs, much more of the increase in residential rates would flow to business rates. But any reduction in local business rates should have the same (positive) effect on consumer welfare as reductions in business long-distance rates because these reductions would also flow through to consumers in the form of lower consumer prices.

Why Is Such an Inefficient Policy So Durable?

One might reasonably ask why universal service pricing policies persist if they are so clearly inefficient and costly to consumers in general. The answer may have its roots in the "median-voter" hypothesis that is invoked to explain much public policy in a representative democracy.[29] Regulation, at its root, is a political phenomenon whose viability depends directly or indirectly on results in the electoral marketplace. Regulatory commissioners cannot remain in office if their policies are sufficiently unpopular with a large share of voters. In particular, if more than half of voters suffer from a change in policy, such a change may have little chance for political success.

Recall that the benefits from abandoning universal service pricing for a more rational, cost-based system redound to those people who use their telephones most intensively. In our analysis, the benefits accrue solely through increases in the use of long-distance service although a complete analysis would deal with increases in the use of other overpriced residential and business services. Because long-distance use is highly skewed, the benefits of cost-based pricing may also be skewed and, though large, may benefit fewer than 50 percent of households. To show this, we estimate the proportion of households who benefit from cost-based repricing in each of our highlighted four states under the BCPM and HCPM cost conditions. The results appear in table 6-11.

Cost-based rebalancing generally creates benefits for between 40 and 51 percent of the population statewide. In every case, urban customers benefit, and in most cases suburban subscribers also realize benefits. But only about one-third of rural subscribers gain; therefore, in the most rural states the losers in rural areas can outvote those who would gain and prevent the promulgation of an efficient policy. In examining the urbanized states, we find the median voter in New Jersey would not gain under either model and in California would only gain under the HCPM.

Of course, these states already have much more balanced rates than the rural states, suggesting that regulators may have gone about as far as they can (politically) go.

A Concluding Note

We do not purport to have estimated the effects of alternative rebalancing or subsidy programs with total precision. Our estimates for each state are based on extrapolating from the major BOCs' (and SNET's) costs to the entire state. We are forced to do this by the inability

Table 6-11. *Percentage of Households Benefiting from Cost-Based Rate Rebalancing, 1996*

State	Area	BCPM	HCPM
California			
	Urban	50.4	100.0
	Suburban	36.4	17.4
	Rural	7.1	0.0
	Total	41.7	51.3
Mississippi			
	Urban	71.6	100.0
	Suburban	78.7	100.0
	Rural	34.3	34.3
	Total	41.1	45.2
New Jersey			
	Urban	61.9	100.0
	Suburban	37.6	36.3
	Total	40.2	43.1
Wyoming			
	Urban	54.0	66.0
	Suburban	52.0	81.0
	Rural	36.8	29.8
	Total	42.1	47.2

Source: Authors' calculations.

to obtain data on non-RBOC rates. The non-RBOC companies have, on average, a far greater share of high-cost loops. Therefore, we have surely underestimated the welfare costs of the current universal service policy. Put another way, we have underestimated the benefits of moving local residential rates to cost. Nor do we have confidence that any of the cost models is accurate, but no one can know these costs with precision.

These data deficiencies are not likely to detract from the general conclusion of this chapter. We have documented the large cost of traditional universal service policies in the United States and the surprising degree to which residential subscribers in the rural states bear the cost of subsidizing high-cost rural loops. Yet the politics in these very states are often the strongest for preserving these costly subsidies. Moreover, the imposition of a tax on all telecom revenues to cover the costs of these high-cost lines is also inefficient and likely to be very expensive in rural states unless these states can somehow persuade national politicians to levy the same tax rates on urban states and move the proceeds to the rural states.

7 | The 1996 U.S. Telecommunication Act and Traditional Universal Service

The 1996 Telecommunications Act was designed by Congress to promote competition. It requires all states to open their telecommunications markets to entry, including the provision of local access services. While the act's provisions for opening these markets are complicated and have engendered a seemingly endless series of regulatory and legal challenges, the act certainly places the unbalanced rate structures in most states at risk from opportunistic entry. As entry occurs, the current sources of universal service support will undoubtedly begin to be bid away by the new entrants as they attack the urban and business markets, exposing the state regulatory commissions to the need to raise residential rates sharply in areas where they are far below cost.

From Implicit Universal Service Support to Explicit Subsidies

The Telecommunications Act does not provide a remedy for the states' problem directly, but it provides a new approach for the federal portion of universal service support and therefore implicitly provides direction for the states. All existing federal support programs are to be replaced with direct, portable subsidies funded by a tax on interstate and international services.

129

After consultation with a joint board of federal and state regulators, the FCC has decided that the subsidies are to be paid in proportion to the degree to which a carrier has subscribers in areas with forward-looking costs per line that exceed a maximum "threshold" level of affordability.[1] The estimate of forward-looking costs is based on the commission's own Hybrid Cost Proxy Model(HCPM).[2]

The FCC's announced policy does not mention rate rebalancing. Given the 1996 act's admonition to keep all rates "affordable" and "reasonably comparable to rates charged for similar services in urban areas,"[3] the commission sees its problem as one of converting the current implicit system of support to high-cost areas that is buried in the rate structure into explicit subsidies without fundamentally altering the current local rate structure, which it deems to satisfy the act's mandate of affordability. However, it has used increases in subscriber line charges (SLCs) and presubscriber interexchange carrier charges (PICCs) as a method of reducing long-distance access rates and thus implicitly rebalancing rates.[4]

The states could follow the FCC approach and establish a universal service fund that is collected from a tax on all intrastate telecommunications services and paid to carriers in proportion to their provision of service on high-cost lines. These revenues would presumably be offset by reductions in the rates that are currently being used to subsidize high-cost areas: namely, long-distance services, carrier access charges, and business rates. Alternatively, the states could rebalance rates directly and avoid the necessity of levying large new taxes on telecommunications to keep their subsidy programs intact. The latter option is obviously less likely to be pursued by politically sensitive state regulators, even though we have shown that it could redound greatly to the benefit of the average residential subscriber.

A National Direct-Support (Taxation) Option for High-Cost Support

In the post-1996 competitive marketplace, the system of implicit support must be converted to explicit payments for two reasons. First, competitors must be given the opportunity to collect the support payments for serving subscribers at rates that are set below cost for the regulated companies. Second, the regulated companies must be relieved of the necessity to collect the support monies from supracompetitive rates on other services or from other customers. With competitive entry, such sources of support will erode over time, particularly in the more rural states.

The commission could satisfy both objectives by estimating the cost of serving each and every subscriber. For those who are now served at rates below the estimated cost of service, the commission would establish a support, or "subsidy," rate equal to some fraction of the difference between the rate and estimated cost. Of course, such an undertaking would require a monumental effort of regulatory cost estimation that would not be likely to be very successful,[5] but the policy would simply be a nonstarter for another reason: it would require huge explicit payments because the support level would not be calculated by averaging above-cost rates with below-cost rates over a given geographical area. Instead, the commission has decided to average the explicit support calculation over a wide area—a company's operations in an entire state. Entrants, however, will receive support payments based on the average cost of serving subscribers within their given wire centers. A more carefully targeted subsidy system would require much larger "contributions," or taxes, to support it.[6]

It would not be productive to describe and analyze all of the direct-support options that have been considered by the FCC in attempting to implement the universal service provisions of the act. The commission has stated its intent to distribute at least part of the proceeds of the tax—or "contribution factor" in its terminology—on interstate telecommunications revenues to force a reduction in interstate access charges collected by the large local carriers. It delayed its decision on this "high-cost" universal service support for the carriers repeatedly as it tried to resolve a number of related issues involving access charges and fixed monthly subscriber line charges.

How High a Tax?

Before considering the FCC's plan to implement the high-cost universal service provisions of the 1996 act, we analyze the effects of using a general tax (or contribution factor) on all telecommunications revenues as a source of explicit support for high-cost subscribers. To do this, we begin by simulating the effects of two tax regimes designed to pay for high-cost subscribers. In the first, we assume that a federal tax is imposed on interstate residential services to provide 25 percent of the "high-cost" fund

Table 7-1. *Taxes on Residential Services Required to Fund "Rebalancing" of Long-Distance Rates without Raising Residential Flat Rates to Cost*

Cost model	Uniform tax on all services	Federal tax for 25 percent of required revenue	Average state tax for 75 percent of required revenue
BCPM[a]	0.355	0.220	0.436
CI[b]	0.152	0.085	0.201
HCPM[c]	0.116	0.064	0.154

Source: Authors' calculations.
a. Benchmark Cost Proxy Model 3.1.
b. Common Input model.
c. Hybrid Cost Proxy Model.

and that the states levy an intrastate tax sufficiently large to cover the rest (that is, 75 percent) of the state's high-cost residential lines. In the second, we assume that a single, uniform tax is collected on all residential telecom revenues. In both cases, we maintain the local rate structure but use the proceeds of the tax to reduce long-distance rates to the same extent as described in the rebalancing exercise in chapter 6. In other words, rather than rebalancing local and long-distance rates, we use a tax or a set of taxes to achieve the long-distance rate reductions.[7]

The amount of taxes that must be collected to fund a rebalancing of long-distance rates equivalent to that achieved by raising local residential rates to cost is substantial. We begin by assuming that the tax is levied on a revenue base of residential telephone services provided by local and long-distance carriers to residences. We exclude wireless services and telecommunications services provided in 1996 by competitive access providers (CAPs) and other telecom companies.[8] The tax rates required to effect the reduction in long-distance rates achievable by local rate rebalancing are shown in table 7-1.

Needless to say, these tax rates are staggering, reflecting the enormous distortions in current telephone rates. The magnitude of the required tax varies greatly across the three cost models. The rates are calculated by determining the size of the tax that, when multiplied by the interstate or intrastate revenue base, will produce the requisite revenues. Thus, in the last two columns, even though the intrastate revenue requirement is three times the interstate requirement, the requisite intrastate rate is much less than three times the interstate rate because of the differences in the revenue

Table 7-2. *Welfare Effects of Substituting a Telecom Tax on Residential Revenues for Local Rate Increases to Reduce Long-Distance Rates*

Scenario	Marginal cost assumption for long-distance ($/minute)	Annual welfare gains ($ millions)		
		BCPM	CI	HCPM
Full rebalancing (no tax)	0.04	7,046	4,173	3,273
	0.06	5,479	3,404	2,694
Federal telecom tax pays for	0.04	5,079	2,602	1,826
25 percent of high-cost	0.06	4,055	2,155	1,495
requirement; intrastate				
telecom tax pays for rest				
Uniform tax on all telecom	0.04	4,325	1,966	1,052
services pays for high-cost	0.06	3,481	1,634	832
requirement				

Source: Authors' calculations.

base. Even when one uses the CI model or the HCPM, to reduce long-distance rates by the amount available from the cost-based rebalancing shown in chapter 6 requires average tax rates on telecommunications services in the range of 11 to 15 percent. Such rates would obviously create serious political opposition if they were proposed.[9]

The Effects on Economic Welfare

The results of using overt telecommunications taxes in lieu of the current system are not surprising (table 7-2). By taxing the more price-elastic long-distance services as well as local services, we obtain a far smaller welfare gain from the attempt to lower long-distance rates than from the full rebalancing of local residential flat rates. With the Benchmark Cost Proxy Model 3.1 (BCPM), we find that a combined federal-state tax—with the federal tax rate set at 22 percent and each state's tax calibrated to raise the remaining 75 percent—to pay for long-distance rate reductions generates about $1.4 billion to $2.0 billion less in annual welfare gains than the "full rebalancing" (without a tax) scenario. A uniform federal-state tax of 35.5 percent reduces the welfare gains even more because it taxes interstate revenues (that is, long-distance services) more heavily. The single-rate tax reduces the welfare gains from repricing by about 40 percent.

Similarly, under the CI model, a federal and state tax regime designed to recover 25 percent of the cost from interstate revenues—with a federal tax of 8.5 percent—generates a welfare gain that is about $1.2 billion to $1.6 billion a year lower than that achieved by full rebalancing. Finally, under the HCPM, substituting the federal-state taxes for full rate rebalancing leads to welfare gains that are about $1.2 billion to $1.4 billion a year lower. And a uniform tax of 10.5 percent on all telecom revenues to pay for the HCPM estimate of high-cost loops reduces the welfare gain by another $0.7 billion to $0.8 billion a year. Clearly, taxing all telecom revenues to reduce long-distance charges is not a very efficient mechanism. Nor does it reduce the distortion in local rates—one of the primary goals of the policy in the first place.

These results suggest that any federal program to generate high-cost support through a "contribution charge" or tax on interstate revenues has much more damaging effects on economic welfare than would a tax levied solely on intrastate revenues. The reason, of course, is that 75 percent of long-distance charges are in the interstate jurisdiction; therefore, a federal tax on interstate revenues affects the price-sensitive long-distance services more strongly than an equivalent intrastate tax that falls heavily on the less price-sensitive local revenues. However, reliance on intrastate taxes to support a state's own high-cost loops is more expensive for rural states like Mississippi or Wyoming, which must impose taxes of 30 to 70 percent just to cover their 75 percent share, than for California or New Jersey, which need to impose taxes of only 4 to 25 percent.

One way to reduce these taxes is to extend the tax base to all telecommunications services, including business services and all wireless services. Businesses account for more than half of all wireline telephone revenues, and wireless revenues are growing much more rapidly than are the traditional wireline services.[10] Thus, by imposing a tax on all telecommunications services, the tax rates in table 7-1 can be reduced by more than one-half. However, such a strategy risks an even greater reduction in economic welfare since business and wireless demand are likely to be much more price sensitive than are household connections to the network. Indeed, the demand for these services may be even more price sensitive than is residential demand for long distance.[11] If the problem with the implicit high-cost support program inherent in current universal service policy is that price-sensitive long-distance (and other) services are being used to support residential connections, shifting the source of support to business services, which are likely to be at least as price sensitive as residential long-distance services, is no solution at all. Such a policy simply conceals the distortions in "business" charges that reach the consumer indirectly but cost him or her at least as much as the current program.

The FCC Benchmark Approach

We have not attempted to model the FCC's new universal service funding policy because that policy is still evolving. In 1997 the commission decided to postpone the application of its forward-looking cost methodology for estimating universal service support until 2000 for the larger "non-rural" local companies and until 2001 for the rural carriers. In the interim, it maintained its high-cost universal service program based on historical costs. As it has evolved, however, the commission's application of the HCPM to determine high-cost support for the larger carriers results in very little support. The commission decided to set the benchmark for determining support at 135 percent of the national average cost per line. If a carrier's average cost in a given state is above this level, it receives the difference between its estimated forward-looking costs and the 135 percent benchmark. However, for 2000, the commission has decided to employ a "hold harmless" rule, which guarantees that no carrier will receive less than it received under the old mechanism. The result is that nonrural carriers in only seven states have their universal service payments based on the HCPM, and carriers in only nineteen states receive any support at all. The total of such support payments for 2000 is estimated to be $389 million.[12]

The amount of high-cost support for the smaller, rural carriers continues to be based on embedded costs and dominates the high-cost fund. In 2000, these carriers will receive more than $1.5 billion in explicit high-cost support. All high-cost support is now recovered from a tax on interstate telecommunications services that must also fund the new universal service program for schools, libraries, and rural health facilities. Initially, the commission had attempted to recover the support for the latter programs from a tax on interstate, international, and intrastate revenues, but an appeals court decision has required it to reduce the revenue base for this purpose to the interstate and international revenues of domestic interstate carriers.[13] This reduced the revenue base by more than 60 percent, thereby raising the requisite tax from less than 1 percent of revenues to more than

2.6 percent. This clearly constrained the commission's decision in constructing its high-cost support program. Having locked itself into the status quo for rural company support, it simply could not design a very costly high-cost support program for nonrural carriers. Indeed, even with its modest nonrural program, the combined tax on interstate and international revenues was 5.9 percent in the first quarter of 2000, a level that exposes the commission to criticism for constructing such an expensive subsidy program.

The commission's high-cost universal service program generates no improvement in economic welfare in the short term because it does not affect the structure of rates. An explicit tax on interstate revenues is substituted for per minute access charges with no effect on prices. Were the tax on a mix of interstate and intrastate revenues, there would be some efficiency-enhancing rebalancing of rates, but such a tax cannot now be levied by the commission in light of the appellate court's ruling. The commission has been afforded the opportunity to restructure federal rates more directly through a proposal tendered by a consortium of local-exchange and long-distance carriers, but it has been reluctant to embrace their proposal because it is fearful of the political backlash from raising per line rates and reducing per minute rates.[14] Thus, after more than twenty years of economic research that points the way to more efficient pricing, the commission is unable to pursue welfare-maximizing policies in regulating interstate rates. Its high-cost "universal service" policy is still not in place four years after the 1996 act. Moreover, once in place, it is not likely to solve the problems of distorted rates. The high-cost policy only converts an inefficient implicit subsidy program to a similarly inefficient direct subsidy program so that new entrants may collect some of the benefits in rural areas.

Explicit Subsidies and Competition

The purpose of using direct, portable support payments is to allow new entrants and incumbents alike to use such payments in serving "high-cost" subscribers at below-market rates. But as we have seen, such support payments may have to be very large indeed in some rural states if the state regulatory commissions insist on keeping rural residential flat rates far below the long-run incremental cost.

The effect of the existing retail rate distortions on local competition may be gleaned from the fragmentary data that are available on the extent of competitive local-exchange carrier (CLEC) penetration of the local telephone market. The FCC collects data on the degree to which local carriers have lost local lines to CLECs through resale or unbundled local loops, but it has only limited data on lines supplied by the CLECs' own networks.[15] However, Merrill Lynch estimates that the CLECs had 5.3 million switched lines in service by mid-1999 and that 32 percent of these lines were supplied by their own networks.[16] The remaining 3.6 million lines were supplied through a combination of resale and the use of incumbents' unbundled facilities. The FCC's survey of incumbent local-exchange companies (LECs), however, shows that 88 percent of this loss has been through resale and only 12 percent through unbundled loops. About 40 percent of the resold lines are to residential customers. Although there is no direct evidence on the number of residential customers served by the CLECs' own facilities, most of these companies are using their own networks to serve business customers. Thus it seems that CLECs are serving residences primarily through resale of incumbent local carriers' services. If true, this result suggests that three years after the passage of the 1996 act, only about one-fourth of the 5.3 million CLEC lines are residential and that CLECs account for only slightly more than 1 percent of residential access lines.

An obvious explanation exists for the lack of competition in residential lines: regulated flat rates are so low that no new entrant is interested in pursuing such customers. Only when rates are rebalanced toward cost will these entrants attempt to compete for residential customers. Under the Telecommunications Act, direct, portable support payments are to be used if rates are not rebalanced fully to cost, but will such support payments be sufficient to attract new investment from the CLECs in high-cost rural areas? The answer is probably negative, because of the likely inadequacy and political vulnerability of such support payments.

In some states, the necessary support payments may have to exceed 15 percent of intrastate revenues, even under HCPM assumptions. Without any rate rebalancing, we find that the HCPM requires a 10.5 percent tax on all residential telecom revenues, intrastate and interstate, to fund below-cost residential rates, even ignoring the small rural companies. If the tax is extended to all telecom revenues, it would fall to about 5 percent, but given the adverse reaction to recent FCC decisions to fund the new schools and libraries universal service programs at interstate tax rates of nearly 3 percent, the commission has been reluctant to fund more than a small share of the required high-cost program. High-cost states, such as Mississippi and Wyoming, will find it exceedingly difficult to impose intrastate taxes of 15 to 20 percent to fund the remaining requirement, and most have thus far been unwilling to rebalance rates very much. The likely outcome is an explicit support system that will have to be kept to minimal levels and, therefore, the continuation of the implicit universal service support scheme that we have criticized throughout this book.

Nor would our conclusions be affected materially even if the FCC and the states decided to fully fund the portable support payments required by today's distorted rate structure. Surely, the CLECs would be reluctant to build facilities in residential areas if 15 to 20 percent of all prospective revenues were to be derived from politically controversial taxes on every citizen's telephone bill. These payments, even if imposed initially, could be wiped out or greatly reduced by the single stroke of a regulator's pen or by a single vote of the legislature. In our view, the regulated residential rates must be rebalanced towards cost before competition for residential lines can begin. Surely, the evidence for the first four years of the Telecommunications Act is clear: competition thus far has been largely limited to the overpriced business lines.

A Simpler Approach to Rebalancing Rates

The FCC could choose to strike a blow for rate rebalancing and greater local residential competition without the detailed cost-estimation process that underlies our calculations in chapter 6. A proposal by its former chief economist William Rogerson and Evan Kwerel to simply raise the subscriber line charge (SLC) or the presubscibed interexchange carrier charge (PICC) by a small amount that varies inversely with broad measures of population density would provide a major step in the right direction.[17] Table 7-3 demonstrates the effect of raising these fixed monthly charges by $1.00 to $5.00 a month, depending on whether the household is in a central city, a suburban location, or a rural location. First, if all local rates were simply raised by $1.00 a month through an increase in the SLC or PICC and the proceeds used to lower long-distance rates, almost 50 percent of the benefits of full repricing under the HCPM would be achieved. Rate increases of $2.00 a month in rural areas, $1.00 in suburban areas, and $0.30 in central cities would raise the same amount of revenue and generate virtually the same economic benefits but would obviously increase the cost to rural households. Finally, a set of charges equal to $5.00 a month in rural areas, $2.50 in suburban areas, and $1.20 in central cities

Table 7-3. *Raising SLCs or PICCs to Reduce Long-Distance Rates and Rebalance Rural and Urban Flat Residential Rates*

Policy[a]	Monthly increased charge ($)			Annual gain in economic welfare ($ billions)	Annual cost to rural residences ($ billions)	Annual cost to households with income of $20,000 or less ($ billions)
	Rural	Suburban	Central city			
Full rebalancing (HCPM)	...	...	...	2.7		
Subscriber line charge 1	1	1	1	1.1	0.016	0.016
Subscriber line charge 2	2	1	0.30	1.1	0.012	0.19
Subscriber line charge 3	5	2.50	1.20	2.7	0.031	0.42

Source: Authors' calculations.

a. Assumes marginal cost of long-distance service to be $0.06.

would result in precisely the same economic welfare gains as would full rate rebalancing using the HCPM. Thus a very simple approach to rate rebalancing could solve much of the current U.S. universal service pricing problem if the FCC and state regulators could overcome the political resistance to more rational telephone pricing.

Conclusion

The FCC is on the horns of a dilemma. It cannot provide the necessary environment for local competition in the brave new post-1996 world without first moving regulated rates toward cost. But to rebalance rates explicitly involves either a visible increase in local rates that it cannot force on state regulators or the imposition of an elaborate tax scheme to fund portable subsidies. Neither alternative has much appeal to politically sensitive regulators. This chapter has shown that any tax-support scheme will require substantial tax revenues if it is to be effective. Moreover, the extension of these taxes to business services, which would allow lower tax rates, risks losing most of the economic welfare gains available in rebalancing local rates. The simplest proposal is simply to ratchet up local rates through the current regulatory artifices of SLCs and PICCs that vary by density zone. Whether such a proposal can withstand the opposition of politicians from rural states who seek to continue to tax their urban residents and business and residential long-distance users to keep rural residential connection rates artificially low remains to be seen.

8 | *The New (New) Universal Service*

A s telephone services evolve into more complex tele-communications services, such as broad-band services, Internet access, distance learning, and interactive conferencing services, the discussion of universal service policy shifts to whether subsidies are necessary or desirable for these new services. This debate is not generally carried out in terms of network externalities, but rather in terms of social values. Should we be creating a dual society of "haves" and "have nots"—a society where income differentiates those able to use the new technology from those who cannot?

The general concern of many of these commentators is that participation in the new Information Age requires more than telephone access; therefore, they conclude that these new services need to be subsidized. This concern has now been embodied in the 1996 U.S. Telecommunications Act in the form of subsidized access to the Internet for schools, libraries, and rural health facilities. The cost of these subsidies was initially estimated as about $2.65 billion a year, far more than the traditional federal universal service support for telephony. In France, universal service now consists of the usual telephone services plus an integrated services digital network (ISDN) line and telex services. But are the Internet or broad-band communications services indeed appropriate candidates for a universal service policy?

The Internet

The Internet is a "network of networks," hence the name "Internet." It is crucial to remember that the Internet is not a new infrastructure facility for communicating, but rather a new approach for using the existing telecommunications transmission facilities to communicate. The Internet provides for new ways of sending and receiving information and new ways of pricing compared with traditional voice telephony.[1]

Internet Protocol

The Internet began as an American government initiative to link and to enable communications among distant computers, principally in research universities. Originally funded by the Department of Defense and then by the National Science Foundation, this network between a few computers had to interconnect differing systems and determine how the costs of connection and communications were to be paid. A common communications protocol was developed by the interconnecting groups, called Transmission Control Protocol–Internet Protocol (TCP-IP). This protocol is now in its fifth generation and represents a radical change in the way in which different telecommunications networks interconnect.

First, TCP-IP is an open-network protocol, allowing networks to interface and interconnect without requiring identical or similar operating rules or software. Second, the TCP-IP standard-setting procedure differs significantly from the manner in which the telecommunications sector typically establishes standards for interconnection, and it is also a generic description of how the Internet differs from ordinary telephony. TCP-IP standards have evolved through a voluntary group of users; anyone can provide input into this process via the Internet. Telephone companies set standards unilaterally or have formal vote-taking organizations, such as the International Telecommunications Union (ITU) in Geneva, to set joint standards. The ITU is slow and cumbersome, TCP-IP is not.

Because computers handle digital, rather than analog information, the Internet has been designed to handle bits and bytes, not analog voice signals. Thus a crucial distinction between the Internet and ordinary voice telephony is that the former is just bits of information, whereas the latter is still primarily delivered in the actual frequency of an individual voice. The FCC long distinguished "record," that is, data, from voice communications in its policies. On the Internet, a bit is a bit, whether that bit is an electronic mail (e-mail) message, a travel reservation, or now even a digitized voice signal. On the Internet, one cannot distinguish content; a bit is a bit.

Since all bits are created equal, one cannot price an e-mail message differently from a voice message on the Internet because the system does not know what the bit is. Thus, discriminating by charging more for certain types of originating messages is impossible. On the Internet one cannot easily establish higher prices for voice telephony than for e-mail simply by requiring voice users to pay more.[2] One can, however, charge for priority users, whatever they may be.[3]

A second crucial distinction, and the principal technological innovation of the Internet, is the way in which information is passed along. In voice telephony, when X calls Y, the local loop from X to her switching center, a unit of transmission line, and a local loop from Y's switching center to his phone (Y's local loop) are held open—dedicated to this transmission—for the duration of the call.

An e-mail message from X to Y is not transmitted in the same way. That e-mail message is broken into "packets," each packet is given Y's e-mail address, and the stream of packets is distributed across the Internet. Packets may take different routes and reappear at Y's destination address in a different order than they are sent. However, encoding allows the packages to be reassembled in the correct order. Clearly, for Internet voice telephony, the correct order at the Y end matters. The individual packets are passed across many individual "nets," their path determined by a "router" that searches for open paths and the fastest path to the destination. Because there is no direct circuit set up between X and Y, the time required to deliver the message depends on the slowest packet, and the message is sent as "best available." An e-mail communication between X and Y is not held up because Y is on the phone (that is, Y's local loop is busy), but by busy routes between X and Y.

Because there is no circuit kept open between X and Y for the duration of the call, Internet use is far more efficient than telephony. A ten-page fax from X to Y typically requires an open circuit for two minutes. A ten-page e-mail document sent from X to Y travels along with thousands of other packets and does not require two minutes of its own transmission capacity.

Circuit Switching versus Packet Switching

A critical feature of the Internet is its ability to save on transmission from one switch to another switch. It may also save on local loop time, but not necessarily. To send an e-mail, I must use my local loop, and this use may be exclusive.[4] I do not share it between the Internet and a simultaneous voice call. Thus one Internet voice telephony call of three minutes involves exactly the same two local loops as an ordinary voice call. Typically, all of the potential savings are in the costs of trunk transmission and switching between these two loops.

Robin Mason attempts to measure the short-run average cost—including operating and common costs—of using the Internet for telephony rather than the traditional circuit-switched network.[5] He ignores differences in quality and congestion costs. He concludes that the average cost of a domestic (U.S.) call using the Internet is 6.24 to 8.86 cents a minute. For an international call, his estimate of the cost of an Internet-based call is between 8.32 and 9.2 cents a minute. These are surprisingly large estimates. Mason estimates the cost of an ordinary circuit-switched international call as 8.57 cents a minute. Therefore, he concludes that the attraction of Internet telephony lies not in its lower costs, but rather in consumer avoidance of high charges for domestic and international access required by regulators.

It is likely, therefore, that much of the attraction of some Internet services, such as e-mail or Internet telephony, results not from inherent cost differences between the Internet and the telephone network but from important price differences that are the direct result of regulation, not market forces. Were telephone usage priced efficiently, this attraction would be considerably attenuated.

Initially, the Defense Department and the National Science Foundation paid for the Internet "backbone," that is, the trunk transmission facilities joining the university or research computer networks, and the local networks paid their own costs. Hence, there arose the misperception that the Internet is "free." Obviously it is not. As the discussion above shows, the Internet generally relies heavily on many elements of the telephone system, and someone must pay for those resources.

On April 30, 1995, the National Science Foundation ceased to support the Internet backbone; since then, the Internet has been carried and paid for by private users. Currently a number of providers make up and define the Internet. Within the United States the backbone carriers provide the basic infrastructure. There are thousands of Internet service providers (ISPs) throughout the world who provide Internet service to retail customers. Some of these ISPs are national firms or even global enterprises, such as Compuserve, Sprynet, and America Online. These ISPs pay for the backbone facilities leased from companies such as MCI and for connections to the local-exchange carriers through which they access their customers. Some ISPs are now beginning to invest in their own transport facilities.[6] Indeed, Worldcom is now a major ISP, a domestic long-distance carrier, an international carrier, a major provider of Internet backbone services over its domestic and international transmission facilities, and—through its acquisitions of MCI and MFS—even a local carrier.

Pricing Internet Access

The Internet has traditionally used a very different arrangement for sending and paying for traffic among carriers from the one traditionally employed in sending and settling accounts for traffic among interconnected telephone carriers. For example, in the United States, a traditional telephone call from Miami to Seattle originates on Bell South facilities, is transmitted across state boundaries by facilities owned by AT&T, MCI, or some other interexchange carrier, and is delivered by U.S. West in Seattle. The complexity of apportioning the revenues from the call—"settling," in telecom jargon—among the various carriers has been at the center of U.S. telecom policy for most of this century.[7] For instance, MCI currently bills and collects for a voice call from Miami to Seattle and "settles" with the two local providers at each end, at prices (access charges) well above costs. The Internet, however, utilizes a "bill and keep" approach to settlements— the originator of the message keeps all of the revenues, though it must pay for access to backbone (transmission) capacity.

Internet service providers interconnect by utilizing common interfaces for transmitting and routing traffic in the TCP-IP protocol plus routing software such as Gate Daemon.[8] This commonality ensures that the ISPs are linked and that packets can move between providers. A small ISP's equipment consists of a computer or router, a number of modems, and leased dial-up telephone lines. A large ISP owns or leases private line capacity to interconnect to the Internet backbone. The backbone is the transmission capacity that allows individual users to access sites in distant places or to e-mail colleagues worldwide. Originally, the ISPs, of which there were few, had internal backbones interconnected to one another.[9] Today, ISPs interconnect at Internet gateways, or ADMDs (administrative management domains). As there are few gateways and a concentration of backbone transmission in a few companies, some now fear that large ISPs who have long-term contracts with the backbone gateway providers will be able to discriminate against smaller ISPs.[10]

The rationale for the original bill-and-keep interconnection arrangements between ISPs was straightforward. When an e-mail passed from ISP A to ISP B, both customers benefited (as with a phone call), and each paid its ISP provider.[11] However, an e-mail message is not priced for the time it takes to transit the Internet or the distance it travels. With packet switching, the time in transit is not easily measurable; but for voice calls that keep the circuit open and exclusive to the two parties, the time is easily measured. Furthermore, since e-mail packets can travel different routes, determining the distance or accounting for the different routes is very costly. Hence a one-line e-mail message to a next-door neighbor and a thirty-minute video from Georgia to Geneva incur the same incremental costs (prices) to the sender—zero—and the same revenue flow between ISPs—zero.

It is not at all clear that this system of bill and keep is sustainable. Since no ISP pays for or receives income to transit another provider's system, this billing approach provides the incentive to send messages across everyone else's network but the ISP's own. This leads to congestion for all providers.[12] Second, the cost to users is clearly related to this congestion—the time it takes to have a message received or a file downloaded. Here, clear negative externalities exist. My sending a thirty-minute video from Georgia to Geneva slows down all other traffic, yet I am not charged for this negative externality—particularly if I have flat-rate local residential service and flat-rate monthly Internet service.

Pricing Reform

An important externality for the Internet is the negative externality of congestion. Considerable work is being devoted to developing a pricing system for Internet traffic that will minimize such congestion.[13] A zero price for the incremental message, whatever its length, destination, or urgency, is clearly not the correct price. However, the issue that we wish to address in this chapter is not whether the price should be zero but whether these new services have the externality attributes that would make them candidates for universal service support policies, that is, below-cost prices.

In North America there is another Internet pricing issue that is absent in most of the rest of the world. The United States and Canada generally utilize flat local rates for residential service; a residence pays a flat amount for unlimited local calling. In most countries, local calls are priced, with the price varying by time of day but generally far above incremental cost. A zero price for a local call induces Internet users to leave their computers connected to the Internet for hours without incurring additional charges from the local telephone company, even though they keep a switch port fully occupied, and therefore create costs for the carrier involved. In Europe, however, where all local calls are tariffed, the Internet is creating pressures for new pricing plans, and some carriers are responding by offering large amounts of local connection time for fixed fees.[14]

Internet Usage

In December 1994, when the National Science Foundation still ran the U.S. Internet, 32 percent of total traffic was file transfer (transferring large data or text files from one computer to another), 6 percent was e-mail, and 27 percent information search and retrieval.[15] By September 1999, there were an estimated 201 million users worldwide, with 112.4 million of them in the United States and Canada.[16] In July 1999, there were at least 8.4 million active computer "hosts," that is, information providers who post information or who have web pages.[17] Unfortunately, there are no good estimates of the volume of Internet traffic or its distribution among users precisely because of its "cloud" nature. The major uses of the Internet are still e-mail, file transfer, and information search and retrieval, but Internet voice telephony has begun to grow and is the source of substantial controversy because of the pricing distortions in ordinary (circuit-switched) telephony.

The United States is the world leader by far in computer usage in businesses and in residences. In Europe, the penetration rate for computers per household is about half of that in the United States. Table 8-1 provides recent data on the spread of computers in residences for the United States and a number of other countries. Well over 40 percent of U.S. households now have computers, but only 72 percent of these homes had computers with modems in 1997.[18]

Not all home computer users nor even all of those with modems are currently Internet users. The Census Bureau estimates that 22.2 percent of U.S. households used the Internet at home in 1998.[19] Forty-two percent of U.S. households had computers in 1998, but only about half of those used the Internet. If 50 percent of U.S. households have computers in 2000, 75 percent have modems, and 75 percent of these use the Internet,

Table 8-1. *Home Computer Ownership*
Percent of households

Country	1993	1994	1995	1996	1997	1998
United States	22.8	24.1	...	...	36.6	42.1
Canada	...	...	28.8	...	...	...
United Kingdom	...	16.2	20	25	26.7	31.8
France	...	7.8	10	14	20.2	27.1
Germany	...	14.3	18.3	25.3	33.8	41.8
Italy	...	14	...	...	...	...
Netherlands	...	27	...	...	...	...
Belgium	...	21	...	...	...	...
Denmark	...	32	...	...	...	...
Spain	...	12	...	...	...	...
Ireland	...	18	...	...	...	...
Japan	...	...	15.6	...	...	17
Asia-Pacific[a]	...	...	...	2.1	3.9	5.7

Sources: U.S. National Telecommunications and Information Administration, *Falling through the Net: Defining the Digital Divide* (Department of Commerce, July 1999), p. 17; Eric C. Newburger, *Computer Use in the United States: October 1997*, P20–522 (Bureau of the Census, 1999); *International Herald Tribune*, March 19, 1998, p. 11; *London Times*, March 1998; United Kingdom Office of National Statistics, *Family Spending, 1996–97*, p. 152; *Statistisches Jahrbuch* (1997); Asia-Pacific Media Investor, "The Future of the Asia-Pacific Computer/OnLine Market,"August 29, 1997; Organization for Economic Cooperation and Development, *Information Technology Outlook* (Paris, 1998), p. 88; and Kagan World Media, *"European CD-ROM Market Growth Projections, 1994–2005* (Carmel, Calif.: 1998).

a. Asia-Pacific includes (but is not restricted to) Australia, Japan, Singapore, Hong Kong, India, and China.

then 28 percent of U.S. households would now be using the Internet through their home computers.

Another measure of Internet activity is the number of Internet hosts—the number of machine addresses, including those of suppliers of services or information. Table 8-2 provides OECD information on the number of Internet hosts by country and the number of Internet hosts per capita. In July 1998, the United States had 25.7 million hosts, 75 percent of the hosts in the OECD countries. Canada, Japan, Germany, and the United Kingdom were next, but still far behind, with slightly more than 1 million each. Growth in the number of hosts appears to be accelerating; in the OECD alone the number increased by 24 percent between January and July 1998.[20]

Table 8-2. *Internet Hosts, by Country*

Country	1991	1995	July 1998	July 1998 per 1,000 population
Australia	2,148	40,696	750,327	41.1
Austria	21,774	27,426	132,202	16.2
Belgium	343	23,706	153,760	15.1
Canada	18,582	262,644	1,027,571	34.3
Czech Republic	9,918	63,795	65,672	6.4
Denmark	1,559	36,964	190,293	36.3
Finland	8,761	111,861	513,527	99.9
France	9,290	113,974	431,045	7.4
Germany	21,109	350,707	1,154,340	14.0
Greece	216	5,575	40,061	3.8
Hungary	0	11,298	73,987	7.4
Iceland	194	6,800	20,678	75.5
Ireland	100	9,941	44,840	12.6
Italy	1,656	46,143	320,725	5.6
Japan	6,657	159,776	1,352,200	10.8
Luxembourg	0	1,516	6,145	14.7
Mexico	220	8,382	83,949	0.9
Netherlands	7,382	135,462	514,660	32.9
New Zealand	1,193	43,863	177,753	48.8
Norway	8,264	66,608	312,441	71.6
Portugal	0	8,748	45,113	4.6
Spain	979	39,919	243,436	6.1
Sweden	11,800	106,725	380,634	43.0
Turkey	0	2,790	27,861	0.4
United Kingdom	6,990	291,258	1,190,663	20.5
United States	427,817	4,268,648	25,940,555	95.5
OECD total	566,952	6,440,067	35,473,630	32.5

Source: OECD, *Communications Outlook* (Paris, 1997, 1999).

The Internet and Universal Service

What, if any, are the universal service characteristics of the Internet? To answer this question, we begin with an analysis of the effects of subsidizing Internet services for all households. Then we turn to the three major Internet uses: e-mail, information search and retrieval, and file transfer. We wish to examine whether the original goal of the 1934 Communications Act—

Table 8-3. *Selected U.S. Internet Service Providers, August 1999*

Internet service provider	Type of connection for dial-up services	Dedicated services
AOL	56K	56K
A+Net	28.8K–56K, V90, ISDN	56K, ISDN, DSL, FracT1, T1, FracT3,T3, Frame Relay
Compunet	28.8K, ISDN	56K, ISDN, DSL, FracT1, T1, FracT3,T3, Frame Relay
EarthLink	33.6K–56K, V90, ISDN, Cable	56K, ISDN, DSL, FracT1, T1, FracT3,T3, Frame Relay
GTE Internet	28.8K–56K, V90, ISDN, Cable	56K, FracT1, T1, FracT3,T3, Frame Relay
MCI Worldcom	28.8K–56K,V90, ISDN	. . .
Miraclenet	28.8K, ISDN	56K, FracT1, T1, Frame Relay
Prodigy Internet	28.8K–56K	. . .
Surfcheap.com	28.8K–56K	. . .
SBE Communications	28.8K–56K, ISDN	56K, ISDN, FracT1, T1, FracT3,T3, Frame Relay

Source: www.internet.com [August 8, 1999].

"Make available, so far as possible, to all people of the United States a rapid, efficient, nation-wide, and world-wide wire and radio communication service with adequate facilities at reasonable charges"—requires a distinct public policy, that is, a subsidy for the Internet.

The Cost of Internet Services

As of August 1999, there were approximately 7,500 ISPs in the United States.[21] Table 8-3 lists a few of these providers, their dial-up services, and their dedicated facilities. Clearly, most ISPs now offer numerous services and connection speeds. Households may connect their computers at speeds of up to 56 Kbs using the modems supplied with their computers, or they may arrange for higher speeds through a telephone company (DSL) or their cable television service. Table 8-4 shows the prices that these ISPs offered small customers in August 1999. Most of them offered unlimited access for between $14.95 and $19.95 a month, but this fee is only one part of the total costs of Internet usage.[22] In discussing universal service for

Table 8-4. *Consumer Prices for Dial-Up Internet Services, August 1999*

Internet service provider	Cost per month ($)	Hours included	Cost per additional hour ($)
AOL	21.95	Unlimited	. . .
A+Net	14.95	Unlimited	. . .
Compunet	18.95	Unlimited	. . .
EarthLink	19.95	Unlimited	. . .
GTE Internet	19.95	Unlimited	. . .
MCI Worldcom	16.95–19.95	150	0.99
Miraclenet	18.95	Unlimited	. . .
Prodigy Internet	19.95	Unlimited	. . .
Surfcheap.com	14.95	Unlimited	. . .
SBE Communications	19.95	Unlimited	. . .

Source: Internet.com [August 8, 1999].

telephony, we did not address the price of the customer's terminal equipment—the telephone instrument. Before 1968 in the United States, 1975 in Canada, and 1986 in the United Kingdom, this telephone instrument had to be leased from the telephone service provider, often at a substantial price. For instance, in 1974 a residential customer had to pay $1.25 a month for a telephone handset and only about $6.50 a month for the service itself. Today, a telephone set costs as little as $15.00 to purchase—or about $0.15 to $0.25 a month, to amortize.

For Internet access, a much more expensive instrument is required—a computer with a modem, to allow dial-up access. For e-mail purposes, not much random access memory (RAM) or modem speed is needed. Hence, for e-mail purposes alone, a simple, cheap computer would suffice. Until recently, few manufacturers were targeting that market, but much has changed recently with the introduction of low-cost chips by Amdahl and Cyrus forcing Intel to react.[23] The lowest-cost Internet service is offered by cable companies who retail cable modems for $500. These instruments allow web surfing, and if connected to a printer, printing, but have little memory.

More generally, reasonable Internet access on a computer requires a 486 or Pentium-based machine equipped with Windows 95, 16 Mb of RAM, 1 Gb of memory and a modem capable of 28.8 Kbs speed. Such a machine currently retails for $500 to $800,[24] comes with a three-year service contract and if amortized more than three years at a 10 percent cost

Table 8-5. *Typical Cost of Residential Internet Service*

Item	Monthly cost ($)	Share of total cost	Impact of 10 percent subsidy on total Internet costs
Unbundled			
computer			
and modem	16.00	0.291 to 0.445	−0.029 to −0.044
ISP	19.95	0.363 to 0.555	−0.036 to −0.055
Telephone line	0 to $19	0 to 0.346	0 to −0.035
Total unbundled	35.95 to $54.95	1.00	
Bundled			
computer			
and ISP service	30	0.612 to 1.00	−0.061 to −0.10
Telephone line	0 to 19	0 to 0.388	0 to −0.039
Total bundled	30 to 49	1.00	

Source: Authors' calculations.

of capital, would cost $16.00 to $25.00 a month. An ISP's rate is generally $19.95 a month, and the monthly telephone access may cost as much as $19.00 and as little as nothing each month if the household already has telephone service.

The joint marketing of computers and Internet services now offers consumers a new set of choices. In 1999 CompuServe began to provide a $400 rebate on certain computers if the purchaser would sign up for three years of CompuServe's Premier Internet service at $21.95 a month. The computer could cost $500 to $800; hence, the cost of the computer and Internet service was $100 to $400 plus $790, or $890 to $1190, for three years' service. Other ISPs quickly followed with similar plans, some of which offer a free Pentium computer, new or refurbished, if the purchaser agrees to a two- or three-year Internet service contract at prices that range from $17.95 to $39.95 a month.[25] The lower-priced plans, however, generally force the consumer to view numerous advertisements at each log-in. These new packages signal a decline in the cost of Internet service to consumers. The CompuServe package provides a $400 rebate in return for a customer subscription with a present value of just over $680 to CompuServe at a 10 percent discount rate. Of course, CompuServe obtains other revenues—such as from advertising—that increase with the number of its subscribers.

Table 8-5 provides a breakdown of the costs of various components required for households to subscribe to Internet services in 1999, assuming either unbundled personal computer and ISP service or bundled service.

Once a household has a phone and a computer with a modem, the incremental costs of e-mail are only $19.95 a month and are likely to fall in the near future. At present, approximately 30 percent of U.S. households are in this position.[26] For households with a phone but no computer—approximately 52 percent of U.S. households—the incremental costs of Internet access are $36.00 a month, assuming the purchase of a $500 computer and separate Internet service. For the 6 percent of U.S. households without phones, the incremental cost of Internet access is still $49.00 to $55.00 a month—a very high price for the poor. How would additional "universal access" support for the Internet be provided?

General Internet Subsidies

Current U.S. policy focuses the subsidy on the costs of the communication link, not the ISP bills or computer purchases. Subsidizing the telephone access component by 10 to 50 percent reduces the cost of Internet access and e-mail by 3.9 to 19.4 percent, assuming a $19 local monthly telephone rate and the new low-cost Internet and computer bundled packages (see table 8-5).

How high would a subsidy have to be to increase penetration of the Internet? Recent work by Paul N. Rappoport, Lester D. Taylor, and Donald J. Kridel and by Robert Crandall and Charles Jackson suggests that at a monthly Internet price of zero (instead of $19.95), 55 percent of all households with computers and 75 percent of households with computers and modems would subscribe to the Internet.[27] Assuming that 30 million U.S. households have a computer with a modem and that 75 percent would subscribe at a zero price, the required annual Internet subsidy would cost $19.95 times 22.5 million times 12 months, or $5.4 billion a year, unless one could exclude existing Internet subscribers. This broad-brush policy has been advanced by some, but such a subsidy is apparently not viewed as politically feasible. But then how does one justify the subsidy to telephone connections provided for in the 1996 act?[28]

Given an estimated elasticity of demand (from Rappoport, Taylor, and Kridel) of −0.44 at prices of $20 to $25 per month, increasing Internet penetration by just 10 percent would require a price decrease from $19.95 to $16.07 per month. This price reduction would cost about $46.50 a year for each of the 2 million new households (assuming that there are now 20

Table 8-6. *Distributional Consequences of an Internet Subsidy Designed to Increase Penetration by 10 Percent*

Household income 1996 ($ thousands)	Computer ownership, 1996 (percent)	Internet subscription, 1996 (percent)	Subsidies paid ($/year/ household)
Less than 10	13.1	5.2	2.66
10–15	15.3	4.7	2.40
15–20	22.5	6.9	3.53
20–25	29.3	8.9	4.55
25–35	38.3	10.8	5.52
35–50	50.1	15.4	7.88
50–75	62.5	21.2	10.84
75–100	69.4	26.7	13.66
100 or more	76.4	34.5	17.65

Sources: PNR and Associates, *Request III* (Jenkintown, Pa., 1996); and authors' calculations.

million residential Internet households) or $93 million a year plus $930 million for the households already subscribing.[29] Since households with computers and modems tend to have above-average incomes, such subsidies would obviously be regressive.

We can demonstrate this regressivity by using data on computer ownership and online service subscriptions by income drawn from PNR's 1996 Request III survey. The relevant information is displayed in table 8-6. We assume that Internet (or other online service) subscriptions rise by 10 percent in every income category. Given that computer use rises with income, the probability that a subsidy would benefit those with low income is very low. Only one in every eight households with annual income below $10,000 owned a computer in 1996, whereas three-fourths of households with annual income above $100,000 had computers. General internet subsidies to households are therefore clearly regressive.

Broadband to the Home?

The subsidies for Internet service analyzed above are for Internet usage over a slow, conventional residential telephone line. Recently, there has been a flurry of activity to provide households with higher-speed connections through cable modems, DSL services over telephone lines, and even through satellite circuits. At this juncture, there does not appear to be broad-based support for a new subsidy program for these new high-speed services, but as they spread, the differences between those with the service and the "have nots" will become obvious. The costs of any potential subsidy program for high-speed services are likely to be huge, given that these services are being priced at about 2.5 times the price of a conventional telephone line. We do not have estimates of the price sensitivity of demand for most of these new services because they are so new. Nevertheless, any subsidy program is likely to be even more expensive than the current universal service support program and would be difficult to reverse once it was no longer justified by any externalities or income-redistribution goals it was designed to address.

E-mail

Clearly, there is a positive network externality in e-mail service. The value of the network to me increases as a result of your joining the system. Furthermore, once both of us are subscribers, the marginal costs of e-mailing each other are very close to zero and remain there whether we are in the same local exchange area or on different continents. As a result, a policy of providing below-cost access to the telephone system for those people may be justified. I am better off if I can e-mail you. When you acquire an e-mail address, that is a benefit to me, and one you may not consider in deciding whether to join or not—the classic externality. But too much should not be read into this situation. You would merit a subsidy only if two conditions were fulfilled. First, you do not currently subscribe to e-mail. Second, you would be induced to use e-mail by a subsidy that is less than the externalities you confer on me and others by such use.

A recent Rand study argues that "the nation should support universal access to e-mail through appropriate public and private policies."[30] Several aspects of this issue, however, need to be addressed:

—Is e-mail a substitute for a complement to voice telephony and communications?

—What are the implications of such substitutability or complementarity given that telephone use is generally priced above cost while residential access is subsidized?

—What are the total costs of e-mail and how are they divided between the costs of the required customer equipment and the costs of network access?

—What does a policy of subsidizing the communications costs of e-mail accomplish if these costs are a small share of the total cost of e-mail?

—Are there universal service features of e-mail that require public subsidies?

The existing literature refers to the "obvious" nature of the externalities, but there is no cogent discussion of such externalities.[31] Paul N. Rappoport, Lester D. Taylor, and Donald J. Kridel argue that two externalities exist—network and calling. According to them, "The current torrid expansion of the Net is likely endogenously caused by expansion itself."[32] (This refers to the network externality but also appears to argue that the benefits to connect are so great as to cause a "torrid" expansion. This suggests that much of the externality, is already being internalized.) The "call" externality is the response to an e-mail or site visit, which is another e-mail or site visit. Anyone using the Internet to gain access to data and information is well aware of the ability and incentive to visit other web sites.

One has to be careful in using the word "externality" because to some it may imply a need for a public policy intervention when none is called for. Earlier, we demonstrated the proliferation of refrigerators and VCRs with no public subsidy. Furthermore, while video rental chains rent VCRs, they do not generally subsidize them. The mere fact that services are strategic complements in use does not require vertical integration, subsidies, or public policy intervention. It requires more than the invocation of an externality for a public policy intervention to be justified.

Without access to a telephone, a person has no ability to call someone else. Similarly, without access to a communications line, e-mail is impossible. However, is the telephone a substitute for e-mail or vice versa? If all households have telephones, what is the argument for subsidizing e-mail access? The essential difference is that e-mail does not involve real time communication; it is more like electronically mailing a message for fast delivery to someone else. There is no need for the two communicators to be in simultaneous contact. E-mail also allows a message to be simultaneously sent to many, a form of broadcasting.[33]

So, who are e-mail users? A 1994 study found that 70 percent of e-mail was confined to a closed user group, and only 10 percent was sent between different companies or individuals.[34] This has probably changed significantly. The 1995 Rand study concluded that voice, fax, and e-mail were complementary services but with strong potential substitution. What does it mean if e-mail is a strong substitute for voice calls? It seems to us that the more e-mail is a substitute for existing messaging, the less need there is for public policy. Our reasoning is simple.

We do not know the extent to which e-mail supplants or supplements other services. It is likely that there is some of both. However, a residential telephone line is the dominant form of residential connection to the Internet. Since the price of access is below incremental cost for a large number of residential households in the United States and elsewhere, there already is an inherent "subsidy" to e-mail (and other Internet services). Moreover in North America, there is little measured local service. Hence, a $19.95 monthly payment to an ISP in most U.S. cities is the total cost of unlimited access. Alternatively, a second line to one's home can be left connected to the Internet, twenty-four hours a day, seven days a week for a month for a $19.95 total fee plus the rental of the second line. In the United Kingdom, students have petitioned British Telecom for similar zero-priced local telephone usage, because to gain access to their ISP (through local calls) students can easily run up bills of as much as £200 a month.[35]

Therefore, in the United States and Canada, a substantial incentive already exists to subscribe to and use the Internet—local residential monthly rates that are generally below cost and a zero local call price.[36] The degree of subsidy clearly depends on the long-run marginal cost of a local loop and of switching and local-transport capacity. For instance, at a marginal cost of 0.5 cent a minute, the value of this inducement or "subsidy" from below-cost calling amounts to about $3.00 for ten hours of Internet usage. In European countries, local rates are generally far above marginal cost. For instance, an Internet user in the United Kingdom pays $2.10 an hour for off-peak local calls and $4.80 an hour for peak calls.

Another universal service issue involves the interoperability or interconnection of networks. The 1995 Rand study argues that these universal service issues are in essence addressed by the Internet's open and integrated structure. The Rand study also identifies as a problem the potential lack of connectivity between different networks requiring users to belong to several nets to ensure universal access to e-mail. This was a problem early in the life of the Internet, but the problem effectively disappeared in 1993.[37] "User interest in widely reliable messaging has impelled commercial service providers to establish gateways and develop protocol conversion software. . . . These forces will be sufficient to ensure quite widespread connectivity for basic messaging."[38]

There are many qualitative analyses of the role of externalities in the development of the Internet, but few make any attempt to articulate how these externalities operate or to measure their magnitude. One that does is the 1995 Rand study, which begins with an articulation of the differences between e-mail and telephony. E-mail can be interactive among many; one can broadcast messages to thousands, easily and at low cost; e-mail can be stored and forwarded; it is asynchronous (like postal mail) and unlike a phone call without an answering machine, the receiver need not be home; it is faster than postal mail. However, as Rappoport, Taylor, and Kridel suggest, these advantages of e-mail are perhaps why it is growing rapidly and thus why normal market forces are working. That is, given the extraordinary growth of the Internet, it is difficult to argue that the growth is deterred by the failure to allow for externalities in pricing the service.

File Transfer

Few externalities seem to be present in file transfers. These activities are largely confined to organizations such as universities, research laboratories, and so on, and the benefits of the Internet to these organizations are likely to exceed their costs; therefore, all join at the market clearing price. One organization's file-transfer activity is unlikely to confer unpriced external benefits on others. We see no important policy issue here.

Information Search and Retrieval

The Internet is a marvelous tool for searching and retrieving information. The explosion of web sites has even caused some experts to suggest that there is too much information, in the sense that it cannot feasibly be accessed in a reasonable period of time.[39] Again, there are positive network externalities, but only from the addition of information providers to provide their services. There are, however, no network positive externalities from the enrollment of another Internet subscriber to engage in such searches. The information online is a public good; absent congestion, the information someone accesses does not diminish its availability to a user. However, additional users may degrade access to this information, as my file retrievals slow yours down. This suggests that information providers may be too few because new providers compare the cost of establishing an online site with the private benefits from establishing the service. The network externality argument, as applied to information retrieval, leads to the conclusion that society should subsidize not those who access information but those who provide it. In addition, because information retrieval could well generate external costs from increased congestion, the correct policy is not to subsidize those retrieving information but rather to charge those whose file transfers reduce the ability of others to use the Internet.

Multiple Providers

In its early years, the technological choices for carrying out universal service policy were simple. There was only one technology—the copper wire pair—available for telephony, and that was not useful for other services. Thus universal service for telephony simply involved subsidizing residential telephone service by raising other telephone rates. All of these services were provided by the telephone company. Bypass (that is, substitution of other communications paths for regulated telephony) began to grow, but only slowly. At least the technology—the copper wire pair—was a constant.

If the universal service obligation is now to spread to new advanced services, who will provide the services and how will they be chosen? And, importantly, if differing technologies are competing to deliver a service, is there still a need for a subsidy? Even though the intent is to subsidize Internet access to a variety of institutions, should the subsidy go solely to telephone companies? Now that the Internet can be accessed through a variety of wireless and cable television technologies, surely regulators should allow competition for these subsidies. In this world, prices will be driven toward long-run incremental cost, and the case for continuing subsidies will surely be weakened. Indeed, competition may drive the rates for schools below other commercial rates as Internet-telecom providers seek to encourage students to become users at home.

Universal Access Support for Schools, Libraries, and Hospitals

With the passage of the 1996 act, U.S. universal service policy—the "new new universal service"—now provides subsidies for schools, libraries, and certain rural health service facilities. A joint state-federal board, set up in late 1996, established the support mechanism for Internet access for schools and libraries and lower telecom bills for rural health providers, as well as the ground rules for the high-cost support program for traditional voice services. The FCC rules implementing these universal service provisions have established the subsidy levels for eligible schools, libraries, and rural health facilities. For schools and libraries, these subsidies range from 20 percent to 90 percent of all telecommunications services, Internet access, and inside wiring. Total support is capped at $2.65 billion a year. It was scaled back to about $1.4 billion for the first year of implementation, 1998, and was subsequently increased to $1.98 billion for 2000.[40]

These new universal service policies are designed to increase the number of telephone lines used by each of the eligible facilities, since each computer connecting to an ISP (at the same time) requires a telephone line. These subsidies have already become controversial because they are assessed as indirect taxes on interstate and intrastate carriers who now threaten to list them explicitly on consumers' bills. Furthermore, large, new bureaucracies were initially established to administer the programs, but political pressure has forced the FCC to scale back these costs. The program is administered by a new universal service administration company. The FCC has also faced challenges as to how it spends the monies, as not surprisingly, the demand for funding quickly exceeded the cap.[41]

The sums involved—about $2.0 billion a year—are approximately equal to the explicit transfers for the other parts of the universal service program. How are the subsidies established and how are the funds raised?

Table 8-7 provides the discount matrix that is to be applied to "the lowest price charged to similarly situated non-residential customers for the same type of services" for schools. The discounts are based on one of two criteria. As shown in this table, they may be based on the percentage of students in the school eligible for subsidized school lunches, a measure of students in poverty. Alternatively, a school can use Title 1 of the Improving Schools Act of 1994 to determine the discount.[42]

The discount ranges from 20 percent for urban schools serving the children of the rich, to 90 percent for schools where 75 percent or more of the students are eligible for state-supported school lunches, and 80 percent for schools where more than half of the students receive school lunches. By these rules, 32 percent of all U.S. schools receive at least an 80 percent subsidy, and about 68 percent receive a discount of at least 50 percent.

We do not know how the matrix was arrived at, but it is extremely unlikely that the differential in discounts between any two categories is designed to offset the difference in the probability of having sufficient telephone line subscriptions. Nor is there any motivation for offering wealthy schools a 20 to 25 percent discount. Moreover, the program does

Table 8-7. *Universal Service Fund Subsidy Rates for Schools*

School lunch eligibility (percent)	Share of U.S. schools	Percent discount for urban location	Percent discount for rural location
Less than 1	0.03	20	25
1–19	0.31	40	50
20–34	0.19	50	60
35–49	0.15	60	70
50–74	0.16	80	80
75–100	0.16	90	90

Source: www.merit.edu/usf/newregs.html [March 7, 2000].

not address the costs of computers for schools, of suitable teachers, or of other required infrastructure. It is difficult for a politician (or a regulator) to stand against "Internet for Kids," but the question is whether up to $1.98 billion a year spent this way is the best use of society's resources.[43]

These new subsidies for schools, libraries, and rural health services are directed at the Internet, not at computer use. Internet access may well be an important social issue, and computers in schools may be vital to educating everyone. But focusing attention only on the communications link tends to distract from the important issues of optimal deployment and financing of the entire package—computer, computer education, Internet service, and communications link. Why should the communications link and the Internet service be the central focus of this type of "universal service"? And who should fund the subsidy for this service? If the entire package is important to society and is subject to externalities, why should telecom users or long-distance callers be asked to subsidize the communications link that helps to improve education or health care? Should computer manufacturers be asked to fund the computer component through a tax on computer sales, or should ISPs fund the Internet with a tax on the requisite online services?[44]

Education is clearly a crucial service, and Internet access to schools may be a valuable component of educational policy. Nevertheless, it would be reasonable to conclude that the optimal mix of teachers, buildings, books, and Internet connections is best determined by those making education policy decisions. Surely, the optimal mix differs across schools. As a result, it seems particularly unwise to have uniform subsidies for such a narrow component of the education-input package. Equally important, taxing a narrow group of products with fairly price-elastic demand—such as telephone calls—to subsidize broad policy goals is highly inefficient.

It is hardly surprising that schools have been able to connect to the Internet without any subsidy program administered in Washington. By the autumn of 1997, fully 78 percent of all public schools had access to the Internet, up sharply from just 35 percent in 1994.[45] This penetration was achieved without the new new universal service policy, which did not begin until 1998. Nor has public school access to the Internet accelerated since the FCC ruled on eligibility of various expenditure categories for federal subsidies. Chairman William Kennard stated that the e-rate helped raise the level of access to the Internet, since 80,000 schools and 38 million children were helped by the program.[46] However, no analysis has been done to show which schools linked up because of the subsidy. In short, the schools appear to have been on their way to developing Internet access without the assistance of a new telecommunications subsidy program.

Using the model developed in chapter 7 for examining the implications of traditional universal service policy, we can demonstrate that funding this program with a tax on all telecom services is less economically efficient than funding it from a tax on telephone lines or—as Jerry Hausman has shown—on general revenues. The annual cost of the new universal service policies for schools, libraries, and rural health facilities is generally assumed to be in the range of $2.5 billion to $3.0 billion a year. However, the FCC is currently only funding the programs at a rate of $1.98 billion a year, even though the "demand" for funds had been projected by the program administrators at $2.86 billion a year.[47] If the $1.98 billion were raised from a tax solely on residential telecom revenues—interstate and intrastate—the tax rate would have to be 7.4 percent and would reduce economic welfare by $3.0 billion to $3.7 billion a year under our model assumptions, or by $1.0 billion to $1.3 billion over and above the revenue yield of the program.[48]

Were the tax reduced and extended to all telecommunications services, including business and wireless services, the excess cost could rise greatly because of the effect of taxing services with more price-elastic demand. Of course, it is too early to know if these Internet subsidies generate benefits to the economy that are as great as the tax revenues generated to fund them or, more important, as great as the burden that these taxes place on the overall economy. Our concerns are that these studies will never be done and that the e-rate will be a permanent part of universal service subsidies for decades to come.

Conclusions

We have shown that universal service has been provided by market forces for many goods and services. For telephony, the policy of promoting access to the fixed-line telephone network has resulted in prices for using the network being set above costs. For people who use the phone little or for those whose costs of access are very high, this subsidy and tax scheme is beneficial. But for many telephone users, this scheme lowers economic welfare as they are taxed to support others. Our research shows that those who live in highly rural states suffer the most; in these states, access costs are high, universal subsidies are high, and all users are taxed heavily in proportion to their long-distance calling, thus lowering calling inefficiently. Maintaining subsidies but paying for them with explicit taxes on revenues is also inefficient, since the tax falls on highly elastic services—calling.

When one examines new communications services—such as those offered over the Internet—and asks whether these are worthy of universal service subsidies, two critical issues emerge. The first is whether a subsidy is required for access to these services to encourage efficient exploitation of externalities. The second is the cost of the subsidy and how it would be collected. While the growth of the Internet has been explosive, there is a possibility that low-income households will not become users because of the cost of a computer and the monthly cost of Internet access. Both computer equipment and Internet access are supplied by competitive markets and are not targets for universal service policies. But subsidizing only the communications link will do precious little to encourage low-income Internet subscription.

Of the major uses of the Internet, only e-mail displays any traditional externalities, and even for this use the availability of substitutes—such as the telephone—reduces the social importance of every home having an e-mail address.

Recent U.S. public policy does promote Internet access to schools, libraries, and rural hospitals at a cost that is currently $2 billion. Adding subsidies for Internet access to the poor would increase this amount. Raising the monies for this subsidy is now accomplished by taxing telecom customer revenues even though Internet access in schools and hospitals is less communications policy than education and health policy. Taxing the revenues of telecom firms for these purposes is clearly inefficient and even somewhat inequitable. A tax of this magnitude reduces welfare by $3.0

billion to $3.7 billion a year. If these subsidies are desirable public policies, let the monies be raised by increasing education and health budgets. In addition, since Internet traffic can also be carried by other infrastructures—for example, cable—taxing only telecom and not cable unfairly increases the competitive ability of cable. Therefore, we recommend that these subsidies be raised in more competitively neutral, equitable, and efficient ways by placing them directly in the budgets of educational and health services.

9 | *The Need for a More Focused Policy*

We have shown that the objectives of and the justification for a universal service policy in regulating the telephone industry have changed over the twentieth century, especially in the United States. While most OECD countries have had some form of implicit universal service pricing policy, many are now moving away from such policies as they open their telecommunications sectors to competition. Prices that do not reflect incremental cost cannot survive in a competitive market. The United States, however, continues to administer a costly and even expanding policy that is beginning to embrace new services, using a taxation scheme rather than implicit subsidies to support new universal service programs.

At first, universal service was the justification—excuse?—used by AT&T for promoting an interconnection policy that would lead to a single, monopoly network.[1] While the 1934 U.S. Communications Act embraced the notion of universal access of telephone services, only when external threats to AT&T's monopoly developed in the long-distance market was universal service transformed into a policy of keeping the prices of residential connections—particularly in rural "high-cost" areas—below incremental cost. These below-cost connections were paid for by supracompetitive pricing of business connections, residential connections in large urban areas, and especially long-distance service, interstate and intrastate. This latter policy survives to this day in the United States as in most countries, but it is now under enormous pressure owing to the liberalization of entry.

The recent shift to an explicit direct system of supporting universal telephone service in high-cost areas in the United States was initially accompanied by an expansion of the objectives of the program. Universal service was extended to public institutions—schools, libraries, and rural health centers—and from simple telephony to advanced (high-speed) telecommunications services. Once a largely hidden policy of shuffling rents from the more intensive users of the network, and from urban and business subscribers, to less intensive residential users, U.S. universal service policy has become a growing, visible policy of overt taxation and redistribution carried out by telecom regulators. As a result, the policy has appeared on political radar screens and has come under attack. To some, this may seem unfortunate, but given the incredible inefficiency of universal service policies in recent decades, we view this environment as a healthy one in which to discuss major changes in the U.S. program. In many other OECD countries, this debate is rapidly being resolved in favor of a sharp reduction in cross-subsidies.[2]

What Are the Goals?

Maintaining affordable, ubiquitous telephone service is no longer just a policy goal in almost every developed country; it is an immutable reality. In the United States, 94 percent of all households subscribe to telephone service; in Canada, 98 percent subscribe. Moreover, all of the recent econometric research demonstrates that the decision to subscribe is extremely price insensitive. Even a doubling of local rates (line rentals) would only reduce residential subscribership by 1 to 3 percent at most. In our demand estimates for the United States, we cannot detect any price sensitivity for the average household at current rates for the monthly bill. A high once-for-all fee to connect to the system does have an appreciable but small effect on low-income households' decision to have a phone.

The goal of affordable, ubiquitous telephone service can only have meaning if one defines "affordability." Clearly, in the United States and Canada, where the average household spends less than 1 percent of its income on local telephone service, the issue of affordability must be moot—at least to the average household. In these countries, households, on average, spend more on toiletries than on telephone connections. Moreover, since subscriptions and purchases of other services such as television, VCRs, and cable television approach near universality without any subsidy, why is telephone service alone deserving of a subsidy?

We are left with only two possibilities for even considering a policy of reducing the price of telephone connections below their efficient, cost-based levels: encouraging low-income nonsubscribers to join the network or pure income redistribution. We have seen that telephone subscription is lower among poor households and among black and Hispanic U.S. households regardless of their income. It might be desirable to attempt to increase poor households' subscriptions to telephone service, but one should be cautious in concluding that such a policy would be as valuable to the recipients as alternative uses of the subsidy monies. The recurring theme of this book is that universal service policies are a very imprecise system of income redistribution and have large costs in economic welfare.

Alternatively, many politicians may see universal service policy as a way of redistributing income from those who happen to live close to a telephone switching office to those very far away from one. Urban subscribers—residential and business—are taxed to pay for high-cost rural connections presumably because there is a notion that it is unfair to penalize people with prices that reflect the cost of getting services to their more remote areas. Uniform postal service pricing presumably derives from a similar notion. However, we found that there is generally no such policy for other "utility" services in the United States. Even the rural electricity subsidy is small and it is being reduced over time. Moreover, it is far from clear that rural households should be the object of sympathy compared with their urban brethren. The higher costs of congestion, pollution, and housing for residents of more densely populated areas surely offset the higher costs of connecting to wires or pipes in rural areas. Why should policymakers try to equalize the prices of one of these services across the country?

Finally, new, innovative services must be addressed. In chapter 8, we reviewed the arguments for providing subsidies to induce subscriptions to new services to capture the benefits of network externalities. We showed that most of these new telecom services involve some aspect of using the Internet. Unfortunately, these services are evolving so rapidly that a political decision to direct subsidies toward such a service may be too late or prove misguided.[3] France's decision to subsidize the Minitel and U.S.

proposals to subsidize a fiber-optics-based "information superhighway" are examples of this problem. In France, Internet usage lagged the rest of the West because of policymakers' attempts to protect the low-speed Minitel system.

Moreover, telecommunications costs are often only a small part of many new information services. Even if we could identify the services for which there may be large unexploited network externalities to be harvested—such as e-mail—subsidizing the telecommunications link that delivers them may be rather ineffective because the major barriers to the ubiquity of such services are computer ownership and computer literacy. Reducing the price of the telecommunications link to the computer might simply confer rents on those already using the service, who are largely high-income individuals, without increasing the diffusion of such services.[4]

These various complications suggest a careful elucidation and targeting of any universal service policy. Any subsidies should be directed at

—low-income individuals or households, particularly those who would not choose to subscribe at cost-based prices;

—areas where network connections are so costly as to impose a true hardship on lower-income households or individuals;[5] and

—new services that display significant network externalities and in which cost-based telecommunications charges have a significant impact in slowing the diffusion of the services.

The Source of the Subsidies

Societies use tax revenues for many services. In some cases, the source of the revenue for the subsidy is tied closely to the service being paid for or subsidized. User fees are an obvious example. The U.S. motor fuel tax is another.[6] Taxes on telecom services, whether explicit or implicit, can hardly be characterized as user fees of the traditional variety. They do not provide a source of revenues to provide for necessary infrastructure that cannot be, or is not, provided in the private market. Rather, such taxes are sources of funds to allow the public (or private) telecom carrier to keep the prices of certain services below cost. Taxing certain (or even all) telecommunications services to subsidize specific services or specific households' use of these services is fraught with the danger of reducing economic welfare in the taxed services by more than the benefits derived from the subsidized service. Certainly, taxing price-sensitive telecom usage to subsidize very price-inelastic local connections is an example of this problem.

Our analysis in chapters 3, 6, and 7 shows that the implicit taxes on long-distance services are an inefficient source of subsidy monies and even a somewhat inequitable one, given the skewed distribution of long-distance usage in every income category. Clearly, a tax (or "contribution factor") levied on U.S. interstate telephone services suffers more from this problem than does a similar tax on intrastate services, which are dominated by the less price-elastic local services. We would, however, suggest that any decision to tax telecommunications for the purpose of subsidizing households or new services should be carefully weighed against the alternative of using general tax revenues for this purpose. Use of general revenues would also shift the choice of recipients from the telecom regulators to the legislature—a shift that conforms with the view that such political decisions should be kept from "independent" regulators.

Perhaps a tax on telecom services would be appropriate for subsidizing incremental subscriptions to new services if the external benefits from such additional connections were correlated with the use of other telecom services. We are frankly at a loss to suggest a general rule for identifying such a correlation or—more important—for persuading legislators that such a correlation is a requisite of sound tax policy.

The Impact of Liberalization

We are convinced that a substantial reduction in universal service support levels would be desirable in most countries, particularly in Canada and the United States. Even in rural areas in these two countries, many telephone users are likely to suffer from the policies now in place. Although legislators and regulators may not be convinced by the power of the economic logic that considers such support programs ineffective and inefficient, they are now moving rapidly away from them because they realize that competitive markets cannot support a distorted rate structure. In the European Union, the use of implicit cross-subsidies to support universal service is being severely discouraged by the European Commission. Canada has finally moved rather aggressively to rebalance rates toward costs.

In the wake of the 1996 U.S. Telecommunications Act, the Federal Communications Commission (FCC) is in the midst of a slow, agonizing process of converting its implicit support program to one of explicit subsidies to high-cost connections through a tax on interstate telecommunications revenues. This move is necessary to allow retail rates for telecom services to be "rebalanced"—that is, moved toward their relative costs—as local markets are opened to competition. The states have shown much less interest in rate rebalancing, but as the new competitive local-exchange carriers (CLECs) take a larger and larger share of business lines and high-usage residential lines from incumbents, the state regulators will also have to allow rates to move toward costs. This, in turn, will require that universal service support at the state level be paid explicitly to the carriers or the targeted subscribers from general taxes or taxes on intrastate calling telecom revenues.

Unfortunately, the struggle over the rules spawned by the 1996 Telecommunications Act, the large investments required to enter local markets, and technological uncertainty have combined to generate a very slow pace for local-market competition in the United States. The new competitors are attracting subscribers at a rate of about 2.8 million lines a year, or about 1.6 percent of all access lines, but the rate is accelerating.[7] Moreover, the incumbent local-exchange carriers (LECs) are still expanding through the growth in business and residential lines induced by a strong economy. Thus, state regulators are not yet being forced to confront their universal service subsidy policies.

The experience of the FCC in shifting from implicit to explicit universal service support policies is at least mildly encouraging because it has required the commission to provide justification for a policy designed to shift several billion dollars a year among telecommunications users. The commission initially attempted to persuade interstate carriers that they should not list the universal service taxes as explicit items on their customers' bills, a proposal that was vigorously objected to by one commissioner.[8] In addition, the funds allocated for the new schools, libraries, and rural health support systems have already been reduced in the face of mounting pressure from Congress and members of the FCC.[9] This pressure would not have developed in debates over earlier subsidies, which were hidden in cost allocation and pricing of local carriers' interstate access services. Given that the commission is already collecting about $4.5 billion in taxes to support the various universal service programs without having yet completed its high-cost program for rural companies, it will be under substantial pressure to tailor the various components of these programs to the needs of constituent groups, so as to keep the explicit costs—and the interstate tax rate ("contribution factor")—from rising far above its current 5.9 percent rate.

Suggestions for Shrinking the Universal Service Programs

Clearly, no real economic need exists for maintaining the extensive distortions now built into the rate structures of most developed countries, particularly those of the United States and Canada. In the United States the shift from implicit universal service support, buried in the rate structure, to explicit subsidies to be offered to individual subscribers or to carriers provides the opportunity for the country as a whole and the states to begin to move away from the universal service policies of the past and to target subsidies on those who may have a real need for them. This objective would not include every household in rural areas regardless of its income.

Like most economists, we prefer telephone subsidies to be conferred on low-income persons in high-cost areas. In dense urban areas, there is little need to reduce the price of accessing or using the network below its already inconsequential level of less than $20 a month in most states. However, one might wish to reduce the price of connecting or reconnecting to the network for low-income households with troubled credit histories. These reductions could be combined with various long-distance blocking programs that prevent the inadvertent accumulation of large monthly bills.[10]

Any attempt to reduce support levels in rural areas would have to be phased in by politically sensitive regulators. This could be accomplished by slowly shifting the support payments from the telephone companies to their customers. In the process, this would expose the fact that wealthy farmers or owners of vacation homes are recipients of this largesse. Slowly, the support levels could be reduced by targeting only low-income households. We do not believe that even these payments are necessary to attract more low-income households to the network, nor to keep those that currently subscribe, given the demand estimates in chapter 5, but at least a social equity case can be made for keeping the subsidies for these households.

The current U.S. experiment with the Internet should be allowed to unfold. We find little reason to tax other telecom users to support high-speed lines for schools and libraries and we are confident that future research will show that these subsidies were wasteful or redundant. Schools and libraries can purchase their own telecom services from their traditional funding sources, and they should be asked to trade off these expenditures against spending on teachers' salaries, books, desks, and blackboards. But we caution against any attempt to provide support or subsidies for new services for the "have-nots." No one can be sure whether today's new service will turn out to be as useful as e-mail or as forgettable as the CB radio, the Minitel, or even Beanie Babies.

Notes

Chapter One

1. For a discussion of the commitments made by WTO signatories, see WTO, "Telecommunications Services," S/C/W/74 (Geneva, December 8, 1988).

2. FCC, "Report and Order in the Matter of International Settlement Rates, 1B Docket 96–261," FCC 97–280, August 18, 1997.

3. Lars-Hendrik Roller and Leonard Waverman, "Telecommunications Infrastructure and Economic Development: A Simultaneous Approach," *American Economic Review* (forthcoming).

4. See chapter 5 in this volume.

5. See chapter 2 in this volume.

6. See our discussion of e-mail in chapter 8.

7. See chapter 8.

8. This new subsidy program was added as a rider to the 1996 Telecommunications Act through the Stowe-Rockefeller-Exon-Kerrey provisions, incorporated as section 254(h) of the act. These provisions are being implemented by the Federal Communications Commission and a Federal-State Joint Board. FCC, "Report and Order in the Matter of Federal-State Joint Board on Universal Service, CC Docket 96–45," FCC 97–157, May 8, 1997.

9. We address this point more thoroughly in chapter 2.

10. The same cannot be said for VCRs and washing machines.

11. Milton L. Mueller, *Universal Service: Competition, Interconnection and Monopoly in the Making of the American Telephone System* (Cambridge: MIT Press and AEI Press, 1997).

12. The Bell Company, or American Bell, was the predecessor to the American Telephone and Telegraph Company (AT&T), which survives to this day as the largest long-distance carrier in the United States.

13. Gerald W. Brock, *The Telecommunications Industry: The Dynamics of Market Structure* (Harvard University Press, 1981), chap. 4; and Mueller, *Universal Service.*

14. Mueller, *Universal Service,* p. 7.

15. Ibid., p. 7.

16. Ibid., p. 96.

17. See the following discussion and chapter 2.

18. Census Bureau, *Historical Statistics of the United States, Colonial Times to 1970: Part 2* (Washington, 1975), table R1–12.

19. Mueller, *Universal Service,* pp. 158–59.

20. Robert W. Crandall and Leonard Waverman, *Talk Is Cheap: The Promise of Regulatory Reform in North American Telecommunications* (Brookings, 1995).

21. Long-distance competition was spurred in part by major technological changes in long-distance service that reduced costs dramatically. Similar cost reductions did not occur in ordinary local telephony, and they have not occurred to this day.

22. "Private lines" were dedicated telephone circuits that allow businesses to connect only their own facilities. They were not connected to the telephone company's switch in a manner that allowed the user to access ordinary, switched telephone service.

23. See chapters 3 and 6.

24. FCC, Common Carrier Bureau, *Monitoring Report,* CC Docket 98–202, June 1999, table 7.14.

25. Interstate access charges have been falling for the past fifteen years, in part because the FCC imposed a fixed monthly subscriber-line charge on residential and business lines as a means of shifting the recovery of non-traffic-sensitive costs from per minute charges. In 1997, the FCC further reduced access charges in its Access Charge Order, but they remain substantially above incremental cost. FCC, "First Report and Order in the Matter of Access Charge Reform, CC Docket 96–262," FCC 97–158, May 16, 1997.

26. To an economist, many of these transfers may not constitute a "cross-subsidy" in a strict sense because a subsidy exists only when the source of the subsidy is charged prices that are above stand-alone costs and the subsidized service is sold at a rate that is below its marginal cost. See Gerald R. Faulhaber, "Cross Subsidization: Pricing in Public Enterprises," *American Economic Review,* vol. 65 (December 1975), pp. 966–77. However, there is evidence that cross-subsidies exist in local telephone tariffs. See Karen Palmer, "A Test for Cross-Subsidies in Local Telephone Rates: Do Business Customers Subsidize Residential Customers?" *Rand Journal of Economics,* vol. 23, no. 3 (1992), pp. 415–31.

27. This policy was changed when the FCC converted its high-cost support policies to a system of explicit, transferrable payments funded from a tax on interstate services. See chapter 7.

28. There were differences in these subsidy levels across states because of various state-administered low-income programs.

29. FCC Commissioner Harold Furchtgott-Roth, "Dissenting Statement Re: Federal-State Joint Board on Universal Service, Report to Congress, CC Docket 96–45," April 10, 1998.

30. A federal appeals court has ruled that the FCC may not tax intrastate revenues. *Texas Office of Public Utility Counsel v. FCC*, 183 F. 3d 393 (5th Circ. 1999).

31. FCC, "Seventh Report and Order and Thirteenth Order on Reconsideration in CC Docket 96–45l, Fourth Report and Order in CC Docket 96–262 and Further Notice of Proposed Rulemaking," FCC 99–119, May 28, 1999.

32. FCC, "Proposed Fourth Quarter 1999 Universal Service Contribution Factor for November and December 1999, CC Docket 96–45," DA 99–2109, October 8, 1999; and FCC, "Common Carrier Bureau Releases State-By-State Universal Service High-Cost Support Amounts for Non-Rural Carriers and Forward-Looking Cost Model Results," DA 99–2399, November 2, 1999.

33. FCC, "Recommended Decision in the Matter of Federal-State Joint Board on Universal Service, CC Docket 96–45," IFCC 96J-3, November 8, 1996. The initial funding has since been reduced; see chapter 8.

34. FCC, "Report and Order in the Matter of Federal-State Joint Board on Universal Service, CC Docket 96–45," FCC 97–157, May 8, 1997.

35. FCC, "Proposed Fourth Quarter 1999 Universal Service Contribution Factor for November and December 1999, CC Docket 96–45," DA 99–2109, October 8, 1999.

36. See Jerry Hausman. "Taxation by Telecommunications Regulation," *Tax Policy and the Economy*, vol. 12 (1998), pp. 29–48.

37. Crandall and Waverman, *Talk Is Cheap*, chaps. 5 and 6.

38. Telecom Decision CRTC 94–19, "Review of Regulatory Framework," September 16, 1994.

39. Telecom Decision CRTC 95–21, "Implementation of Regulatory Framework- Splitting of the Rate Base and Related Issues," October 31, 1995.

40. These charges were substantially below the access charges in the United States, which averaged 3.8 cents a minute in 1998. FCC, Common Carrier Bureau, Industry Analysis Division, *Trends in Telephone Service* (September 1999), table 1.2.

41. International Telecommunication Union, *World Telecommunication Indicators* (Geneva, 1996).

42. European Commission, Directives 97/33/EC (June 30, 1997) and 96/19/EC (March 13, 1996).

43. European Commission, *Assessment Criteria for National Schemes for the Costing and Financing of Universal Service in Telecommunications and Guidelines for the Member States on Operation of Such Schemes*, COM 96/608 (Brussels: November 27, 1996).

44. The EU approach to universal service was set forth in *Communication on Developing the Universal Service for Telecommunications in a Competitive Environment*, COM 93/543 (Brussels: November 15, 1993); and the *Green Paper on the Liberalisation of Infrastructure and Cable Television Networks: Parts 1 and 2*, COM 94/440 (October 25, 1994) and COM 94/682 (January 25, 1995). It had already been partially implemented through the *ONP Voice Telephony Directive*, COM 95/62 (December 30, 1995). For further details, see also *Communication on Universal Service for Telecommunications in the Perspective of a Fully-Liberalised Environment*, COM 96/73 final (March 13, 1996).

45. European Commission, Directorate General XIII, *Report on Liberalisation* (Brussels: February 1998).

46. EC, "Fifth Report on the Implementation of the Telecommunication Regulatory Package," section 4.5.3, COM 537 final (Brussels, November 10, 1999).

47. Analysys Ltd., *The Future of Universal Service in Telecommunications in Europe* (Cambridge, England, January 13, 1997). However, there is considerable popular support for requiring local carriers to offer flat rate service so as to accommodate Internet use.

48. French Ministry of Posts, Telecommunications, and Space, *Telecommunications Act of 1996*, art. L. 35–1.

49. French Ministry of Posts, Telecommunications, and Space, *Telecommunications Act of 1996*, art. L. 35–1.

50. French Ministry of Posts, Telecommunications, and Space, *Telecommunications Act of 1996*, art. L. 35–2, I.

51. French Ministry of Posts, Telecommunications, and Space, *Telecommunications Act of 1996*, art. L. 35–5.

52. Romesh Vaitilingam, ed., *Europe's Network Industries: Conflicting Priorities* (London: Centre for Economic Policy Research,1998), p. 209.

53. European Commission, Directives 97/33 and 96/19.

54. David L. Kaserman, John W. Mayo, and Joseph E. Flynn, "Cross-Subsidization in Telecommunications: Beyond the Universal Service Fairy Tale," *Journal of Regulatory Economics*, vol. 2 (September 1990), pp. 231–49.

55. Milton L. Mueller and Jorge Reina Schement, "Universal Service from the Bottom Up: A Study of Telephone Penetration in Camden, New Jersey," *The Information Society*, vol. 12 (July 1996), pp. 273–92. See also Jorge Reina Schement, "Beyond Universal Service: Characteristics of Americans without Telephones," *Telecommunications Policy*, vol. 19 (August 1995), pp. 477–85.

56. Frank A. Wolak, "Can Universal Service Survive in a Competitive Telecommunicaitons Environment? Evidence from the United States Consumer Expenditure Survey," *Information Economics and Policy*, vol. 8 (September 1996), pp. 163–203.

57. Ross C. Eriksson, David L. Kaserman, and John A. Mayo, "Targeted and

Untargeted Subsidy Schemes: Evidence from Post-Divestiture Efforts to Promote Universal Telephone Service," *Journal of Law and Economics,* vol. 41 (October 1998), pt. 1, pp. 477–502.

58. See chapter 5 for our attempt to remedy this deficiency.

59. Christopher Garbacz and Herbert G. Thompson Jr.,"Assessing the Impact of FCC Lifeline and Link-Up Programs on Telephone Penetration," *Journal of Regulatory Economics,* vol. 11 (January 1997), pp. 67–78.

60. Jerry Hausman, "Taxation by Telecommunications Regulation," *Tax Policy and the Economy,* vol. 12 (1998), pp. 29–48.

Chapter Two

1. A variety of policies are designed to provide poor people with housing subsidies, food stamps, subsidized health care, and energy assistance, but these policies are not funded from specific, indirect taxes on the same services.

2. Steven N. S. Cheung, "The Fable of the Bees: An Economic Investigation," *Journal of Law and Economics,* vol. 16, no. 1 (1973), pp. 11–33.

3. Ronald Coase, "The Problem of Social Cost," *Journal of Law and Economics,* vol. 3 (October 1960), pp. 1–44.

4. We return to negative externalities in chapter 8 when we discuss the Internet.

5. For a discussion of these externalities and their implications for pricing telecommunications services, see Bridger M. Mitchell and Ingo Vogelsang, *Telecommunications Pricing: Theory and Practice* (Cambridge University Press, 1991), pp. 55–61. It should also be noted that telephone subscriptions may generate negative externalities as more and more persons have the ability to initiate unwelcome calls for everyone else on the network.

6. However, "free" television is paid for by advertisers. Could "universal telephone services" be paid for by telemarketing?

7. Former FCC chairman Reed Hundt often used his eighty-three-year-old grandmother in Kalamazoo, Michigan, as an example of why "universal service" was an important public policy. But Hundt stated that only he called his grandmother. Thus, particularly given his income level, an efficient and equitable solution for the Hundts and society would be for Hundt to pay his grandmother's telephone bill.

8. Lester D. Taylor, *Telecommunications Demand in Theory and Practice* (Dordrecht: Kluwer, 1994), chap. 9.

9. Coase, "The Problem of Social Cost."

10. Except for larger businesses who build their own networks or use large PABXs in lieu of telephone-company lines and switching systems.

11. For our purposes, we would prefer data on the proportion of residential households with telephone service, but such data are not available for a large number of countries.

12. See chapter 5.

13. See chapter 5 for a more detailed econometric investigation of these relationships.

14. The data for total telephone expenditures in table 2-9 include expenditures on cellular and other wireless services. They therefore overstate consumer expenditures on household telephone service.

15. Based on the PNR data described in chapter 3; and PNR and Associates, *Bill Harvesting III* (Jenkintown, Pa., 1996).

16. This will change somewhat now that Canada has reduced its high cigarette taxes to prevent smuggling of cigarettes from the United States and allowed its local telephone rates to rise since liberalization in 1992.

17. For this reason, the FCC now requires states that participate in the Lifeline and Link-Up policies to require local carriers to offer "toll restrictors," arrangements that block households' long-distance calls, when requested.

18. See chapter 5.

Chapter Three

1. We assume that peak costs of terminating or originating calls through the end-office switch are less than one-half cent a minute and perhaps substantially less. See the discussion below and in chapter 6.

2. Average costs are from Federal Communications Commission, Common Carrier Bureau, Industry Analysis Division, *Trends in Telephone Service* (Washington, annual). We use 1996 data in our analysis of pricing and household expenditures in this book. Since 1996, interstate per minute access charges have declined by about 50 percent because of productivity gains and the substitution of per line charges for per minute charges.

3. Department of Commerce, Bureau of the Census, *Annual Survey of Communications, 1996.* Long-distance revenues were $94.0 billion in 1996, and network access charges paid by business firms were $28.5 billion. These data include all types of long-distance services—800 services, private-line services, ordinary switched services, and so on—as well as switched and "special" (dedicated-line) access revenues.

4. We use the term "subsidy" in its popular sense; however, it may even satisfy the narrower economists' definition of the term, in that access charges may be above the stand-alone costs of providing long-distance connections to some subscribers, and residential rates may be below long-run incremental costs.

5. See chapter 1 for a discussion of these programs.

6. Businesses are generally closer to the telephone company switching center, thereby requiring less copper wire per line than do residences, but business subscribers typically have more busy-hour calls than do residences, thereby requiring more switching capacity per line. These two factors offset each other, resulting in rather similar costs for local business and residential service.

7. For evidence on the extent of these cross-subsidies, see Robert W. Crandall and Leonard Waverman, *Talk Is Cheap: The Promise of Regulatory Reform in North American Telecommunications* (Brookings, 1995), chap. 3.

8. This database has been collected by PNR and Associates for a number of telecommunications firms. We have been able to obtain their 1995 and 1996 databases for this study: PNR and Associates, *Bill Harvesting II* (Jenkintown, Pa., 1995) and *Bill Harvesting III* (Jenkintown, Pa., 1996).

9. We do not show these finer income breakdowns, but the data clearly show that once income rises to $30,000, average long-distance spending exceeds all local expenditures, including spending on second lines and vertical features.

10. The 1996–97 edition of the FCC's *Statistics of Communications Common Carriers*, table 2.5, reports that there were 104.3 million residential access lines among the carriers reporting to the FCC. However, the United States Telecom Association reports that the total number of access lines is approximately 108 percent of the FCC's total.

11. They are also likely to subscribe to more "vertical" local services, such as call-waiting, than are lower-income households. Unfortunately, we cannot separate these charges from line-rental charges in the PNR database.

12. We analyze the differential impact on urban and rural households in a later section of this chapter.

13. For estimates of the success of these programs, see chapter 5.

14. Figures 3-3 through 3-5 are derived from the 1996 data in PNR and Associates, *Bill Harvesting III*.

15. If these high access rates are used to suppress some urban residential local flat rates through the regulatory process, the universal-service policy presumably transfers income from intensive long-distance users in all areas to local subscribers even in urban areas. This is not to say that *unregulated* local urban rates would not be even lower, owing to more efficient service from local exchange companies.

16. See Crandall and Waverman, *Talk Is Cheap,* chaps. 5 and 6.

17. The BLS survey does not break down telephone expenditures between local and long-distance charges. However, PNR data show low-income households spend approximately $265 a year on local service.

18. International Telecommunication Union, *World Telecommunication Indicators* (Geneva, 1997), diskette.

19. Obviously, the United States and Canada are much larger countries with lower population density. Therefore, their long-distance rates should be somewhat higher.

20. PNR and Associates, *Bill Harvesting III.* There are no precise data on average price per minute for Canadian long-distance calls in 1992. However, we reported in Crandall and Waverman, *Talk Is Cheap,* chap. 6, that interprovincial rates in Canada were still 30 U.S. cents a minute in 1994 for calls longer than 145 miles. Moreover, Call-Net, a reseller, averaged 28.5 U.S. cents a minute in 1992. See Robert W. Crandall and Leonard Waverman, "Competition in Telecom: The U.S. and Canadian Paths," in *The Electronic Village: Policy Issues of the Information Economy,* edited by Dale Orr and Thomas A. Wilson (MIT Press, 1999), pp. 34–58.

21. The United Kingdom began a price-cap regime in 1984 that permitted British Telecom (BT) to raise local rates slowly over more than a decade. Local rate increases were limited to the rate of general price inflation plus 2 percent a year. This cap was removed in 1996 and replaced by a new price cap that applies to a basket of services used by poorer households. Other retail rates were deregulated. In both countries, long-distance access charges are being reduced by regulatory fiat. In Canada, contribution rates from long-distance services to Bell Canada's territory have fallen to less than one cent (Cdn.) a minute. In the United States interstate access charges are being reduced gradually by substituting presubscribed-line charges for per minute access charges. FCC, "First Report and Order in the Matter of Access Charge Reform, CC Docket 96–262," FCC 97–158, May 16, 1997.

22. PNR and Associates, *Bill Harvesting III.*

23. We assume that the long-run incremental cost of originating and terminating long-distance calls through the local companies' end-office switches is no more than one-half cent a minute at each end. Since access charges are about six cents a minute in 1996, we estimate that they could be reduced by five cents.

24. The Census Bureau reports in the *Annual Survey of Communication Services: 1996* that residential long-distance revenues in 1996 were about $40.8 billion. At an average price of $.162 a minute, this suggests that total residential calling was 250 billion minutes in 1996. Assuming that the demand for long-distance service has a constant elasticity of -.7, a decline in rates from $0.162 to $0.112 a minute would increase long-distance minutes from 250 billion to 324 billion.

The additional calling would generate an additional $0.74 billion in access charges for the local companies plus additional revenues from long-distance services they provide—primarily intra-LATA services. If the local companies accounted for 30 percent of these services and if they yielded another $0.05 to $0.07 cents a minute, the total increase in LEC revenues from demand stimulation would be in the $1.7 to $2.1 billion range.

25. This gain is much smaller than some earlier estimates, including our own (Crandall and Waverman, *Talk Is Cheap*), because we exclude business calls from the calculation and do not address the benefits from greater competition in long-distance services. Nor does this estimate include the effects of the distortions in the *structure* of local rates.

26. Recall that this is somewhat of an underestimate because we have not adjusted long-distance spending levels for the sample months to levels consistent with Census estimates of total residential long-distance spending.

Chapter Four

1. Economists generally use total household expenditures, rather than reported income, to measure ability to pay because many lower-income households have substantial wealth from which they may spend. As a result, average household expenditures are greater than average income for all income groups reported in table 4-1 that are below $20,000.

2. We use 1984 because the Bureau of Labor Statistics changed the methodology of the Consumer Expenditure Survey after the 1983 survey.

3. Bureau of Labor Statistics, *Consumer Expenditure Survey, 1995* (Department of Labor, 1995).

4. Department of Energy, Energy Information Administration, *Electric Sales and Revenue, 1998* (October 1999), pp. 8–9; and Congressional Budge Office, *Should the Federal Government Sell Electricity?* (November 1997).

5. Energy Information Administration, *Federal Energy Subsidies: Direct and Indirect Interventions in Energy Markets* (Department of Energy, 1992), p. 57, table 14. Note that this subsidy is similar in magnitude to the $1.7 billion in annual federal high-cost universal service funds that are transferred to rural telephone companies. But there are far greater implicit subsidies embedded in the telephone rate structure.

6. Energy Information Administration, *Electric Sales and Revenue, 1998* (Department of Energy, 1999), p. 25.

7. Under the 1990 Clean Air Act, areas of the country are determined as "attainment" or "nonattainment" areas based on whether they have met the ambient air quality standards for criteria pollutants.

8. Rural Utilities Service, *1996 Statistical Report: Rural Electric Borrowers* (Department of Agriculture, 1997), p. 15.

9. Bureau of Labor Statistics, *Consumer Expenditure Survey, 1995.*

10. It must be pointed out that this statement is valid only for telephone connection charges—the "local" rates. Large commercial users may indeed obtain telephone service more cheaply than do residences because these large firms can purchase their own PABXs and obtain deeper discounts for inter-LATA long-distance service.

11. Stephen G. Breyer and Paul W. MacAvoy, *Energy Regulation by the Federal Power Commission* (Brookings, 1974).

12. For a more extensive treatment of these phenomena, see Robert J.

Michaels, "The New Age of Natural Gas," *Regulation*, vol. 16 (Winter 1993), pp. 68–79; and Kenneth W. Costello and Daniel J. Duann, "Turning Up the Heat in the Natural Gas Industry," *Regulation*, vol. 19, no. 1 (1996), pp. 52–59.

13. All data are taken from Administration for Children and Families, *Low Income Home Energy Assistance Program, Report to Congress for Fiscal Year 1995* (Department of Health and Human Services, 1997). The most recent year for which data are available is 1995.

14. Jerry Hausman, "Taxation by Telecommunications Regulation," *Tax Policy and the Economy*, vol. 12 (1998), pp. 29–48, shows that the efficiency losses from subsidizing telephone connections from general revenues are less than one-third of the losses from a universal service tax on long-distance services.

15. See chapter 6.

16. The zero-order correlation is 0.25; a correlation of 0.28 is required for statistical significance at the 95 percent confidence level with forty-eight observations.

17. For a history of cable regulation, see Robert W. Crandall and Harold Furchtgott-Roth, *Cable TV: Regulation or Competition?* (Brookings, 1996).

18. The principal impetus came from a General Accounting Office report, *National Survey of Cable Rates and Services*, GAO/RCED 89–193 (August 1989).

19. This result has become controversial. The FCC used a similar result to initiate a "rollback" of rates in 1993–94, but Crandall and Furchtgott-Roth found that the effect of competition disappears for systems within an MSA.

20. Crandall and Furchtgott-Roth, *Cable TV*, pp. 54–55.

Chapter Five

1. National Association of Regulatory Utility Commissioners, *Bell Operating Companies Exchange Service Telephone Rates* (Washington, 1995).

2. The most comprehensive survey of these studies is found in Lester D. Taylor, *Telecommunications Demand: A Survey and Critique* (Ballinger, 1980), chap. 3. He has updated this study in Taylor, *Telecommunications Demand in Theory and Practice* (Dordrecht: Kluwer, 1994).

3. Lewis J. Perl, "Economic and Demographic Determinants of Residential Demand for Basic Telephone Service" (White Plains, N.Y.: National Economic Research Associates, 1978).

4. Lewis J. Perl, "Residential Demand for Telephone Service, 1983" (White Plains, N.Y.: National Economic Research Associates, 1983), figure 5, prepared for the Central Services Organization of the Bell Operating Companies.

5. See Taylor, *Telecommunications Demand in Theory and Practice*, pp. 86–96, for a discussion of these results.

6. Christopher Garbacz and Herbert G. Thompson Jr., "Assessing the Impact of FCC Lifeline and Link-Up Programs on Telephone Penetration," *Journal of Regulatory Economics,* vol. 11 (January 1997), pp. 67–78; Ross C. Eriksson, David L. Kaserman, and John A. Mayo, "Targeted and Untargeted Subsidy Schemes: Evidence from Post-Divestiture Efforts to Promote Universal Telephone Service," *Journal of Law and Economics,* vol. 41, no. 2 (1998), pp. 477–502. See also Leonard Waverman, "Demand for Telephone Services in Great Britain, Canada, and Sweden," Birmingham International Conference in Telecommunications Economics, Birmingham, England, 1974; James H. Alleman, "The Pricing of Local Telephone Service," OT Special Publications 77–14 (Department of Commerce, Office of Telecommunications, 1977); Lewis J. Perl, "Economic and Demographic Determinants of Residential Demand for Basic Telephone Service" (White Plains, N.Y.: National Economic Research Associates, 1978); Lewis J. Perl, "Residential Demand for Telephone Service, 1980" (White Plains, N.Y.: National Economic Research Associates, 1983); Lester D. Taylor and Donald J. Kridel, "Residential Demand for Access to the Telephone Network," in *Telecommunications Demand Modelling: An Integrated View,* edited by Alain deFontenay, Mary H. Shugard, and David S. Sibley (Amsterdam: North-Holland, 1990), pp. 105–17; Jerry Hausman, Timothy Tardiff, and Alexander Belinfante, "The Effects of the Breakup of AT&T on Telephone Penetration in the United States," *American Economic Review,* vol. 83 (May 1993), pp.178–84; and Judith Bodnar, Peter Dilworth, and Salvatore Iacono, "Cross-Sectional Analysis of Residential Telephone Subscription in Canada," *Information Economics and Policy,* vol. 3, no. 4 (1988) pp. 359–78.

7. The average installation fee in our 1990 sample was $189 for the developed countries and $438 for the developing countries.

8. The U.S. Census of Population microdata files do not provide precise geographic identifiers that would allow us to associate local telephone rates with each individual observation. We have had more success with Canadian Family Expenditure Survey microdata (see below).

9. Given that the CPS is based on a rather small sample (approximately 52,000 households out of a national total of 100 million households), the resulting average residential telephone penetration estimates are subject to large standard errors relative to the differences in these averages across states. Therefore, any demand estimates based on these data are likely to be imprecise, though not necessarily biased. See Garbacz and Thompson, "Assessing the Impact of FCC Lifeline and Link-Up Programs on Telephone Penetration," p. 68.

10. In our analysis of 1990 census data we include a second-order term for *POV* to reflect the nonlinear effect of poverty on telephone subscriptions, but this variable did not prove significant in the 1995 CPS regressions.

11. These variables are included to account for the fact that even after accounting for income, these two demographic groups subscribe less to telephone service. This may be due to a variety of societal forces in urban centers. See Jorge

Reina Schement, "Beyond Universal Service: Characteristics of Americans without Telephones, 1980–1993," Working Paper 1 (Washington: Benton Foundation, 1996).

12. See G. S. Maddala, *Limited Dependent and Qualitative Variables in Econometrics* (Cambridge University Press, 1983), pp. 29–30.

13. We do not have flat monthly telephone rates for three states: Illinois, West Virginia, and Wisconsin.

14. For obvious reasons, the *LIFELINE* and *LINKUP* variables for the sub-$10,000 population are not weighted by *POV*.

15. In these regressions, *LINKUP* is a dichotomous dummy variable indicating the presence or absence of the Link-Up program.

16. The linear and semilog results are derived from 1,795 observations, not the full set of 1,897. The 102 observations omitted are those for which the predicted penetration exceeded 100 percent.

17. Attempts to estimate the demand models using simultaneous-equation techniques with relative prices, Lifeline, and Link-Up as endogenous variables were not successful.

18. Tariff data were taken from Stentor publications except for the long-distance rates, which are from Robert W. Crandall and Leonard Waverman, *Talk Is Cheap: The Promise of Regulatory Reform in North American Telecommunications* (Brookings, 1995).

19. Installation charges in Canada in 1992 were very low, ranging from Cdn. $20 in Nova Scotia to $33 in Saskatchewan, but these low rates cannot explain why subscriptions rise, other things being equal, with increases in the rates. A possible explanation is that lower-income, low-penetration provinces use lower installation charges as a means to attract marginal subscribers.

20. Garbacz and Thompson, "Assessing the Impact of FCC Lifeline and Link-Up Programs on Telephone Penetration"; and Eriksson, Kaserman, and Mayo, "Targeted and Untargeted Subsidy Schemes."

Chapter Six

1. Estimating the incremental cost of traditional telephone service in the United States is among the most contentious issues facing telephone regulators in the post–1996 act environment. Unfortunately, there are no *market-based* estimates of these costs because markets have never been permitted to determine costs and rates for traditional service in any country without the guidance of regulators or national governments.

2. The average number of minutes of incoming and outgoing calls per year on a residential line is about 14,000. PCS systems now offer packages of service

for large amounts of calling at prices of as little as $0.10 cents a minute, or even less in rural areas. If a wireless operator were to compete for the right to serve as a residence's primary provider, it would certainly offer inducements—such as free incoming calls or free initial minutes on all calls. Therefore, we view the $100 a month estimate as a maximum value that will certainly decline with advancing wireless technology.

3. These states are chosen to demonstrate the effects of universal service policies in a highly urbanized state and a predominantly rural state.

4. Our analysis uses the HCPM as of July 1999. The specific mapping of the actual locations of subscribers by detailed geographic areas is important for the development of explicit, *transferrable* high-cost universal-service support rates. If subscribers are simply assigned randomly to broader geographic areas for the purposes of estimating costs, the costs of serving some subscribers will be severely underestimated while the cost of serving others will be overestimated. If the support rates are based on such cost estimates, entrants will obviously target the subscribers for whom the costs have been overestimated and ignore those for whom the costs have been underestimated in setting the transferrable universal-service support rates.

5. The ratio of the highest-cost density zone to the lowest-cost zone in table 6-1 is approximately 12 for the Hatfield model, 8 for the BCPM, and 19 for the HCPM.

6. For the HCPM, we use the "geocoded" method of distributing subscribers across the state. This method actually uses survey data on precise household location wherever possible. For the remainder of the state, households are distributed by an algorithm that assigns them within each census block group.

7. Were we to use the Hatfield model, we would obtain larger estimates of consumer welfare improvements because both local rates and long-distance rates would be reduced, but we cannot envision a mechanism by which *regulation* would force such a result.

8. Recent studies suggest limited scale economies in local telephony. (Economies of density are another matter.) Moreover, the continued entry of new carriers into long-distance service suggests that economies of scale in these services are exhausted at output levels that are considerably less than industry output.

9. See chapter 5. This assumption is consistent with recently published evidence (including that in chapter 5) that the price elasticity of demand for residential services is less than 0.01. See Lester D. Taylor, *Telecommunications Demand in Theory and Practice* (Dordrecht: Kluwer, 1994.) We allow for higher price elasticity from lower-income households. Our demand results, however, suggest that subscriptions are unaffected by recurring monthly rates at their current, below-cost levels.

10. Average residential penetration in 1996 was 0.94. See FCC, *Trends in Telephone Service* (September 1999), table 17.1. Telephone penetration is lowest in rural areas and generally rises with income.

11. Estimating the number and location of access lines in each state is a very complex exercise that the HCPM accomplishes through a mix of "geocoding" some subscriber locations and estimating the location of others through a "surrogate" process. Because the estimate of second lines by density zones is difficult to extract from the HCPM runs, we simply use a statewide average of the ratio of secondary to primary lines in each density zone.

12. See James Eisner and Tracy Charles Waldon, "The Demand for Bandwidth: Second Telephone Lines and On-Line Services," Washington, April 16, 1999.

13. This is consistent with the evidence that the overall price elasticity of residential long-distance service is between −0.7 and −0.75. We expect lower-income households to be more price sensitive on average.

14. See chapter 3.

15. Specifically, we raise or lower the estimated average expenditure in proportion to the deviation of the given state's long-distance rate from the national average rate (inter-LATA and intra-LATA) of $0.162 a minute. We do this by allowing expenditures to rise with the formula: $PQ = aP^{(b+1)}$, where P is the price per minute, Q is minutes per month, and b is the price elasticity of demand.

16. We add $2.00 to each rate as a rough estimate of the cost of 911 service and taxes, and an amount equal to $0.005 times the average number of long-distance minutes to price the switching services built into the cost models.

17. Business long-distance revenues are greater than residential revenues [Bureau of the Census, *Annual Survey of Communication Services: 1997* (1998)], and business rates are below residential rates on average. "Affidavit of Robert E. Hall on Behalf of MCI, CC Docket 97–121" (Washington, April 29, 1997) estimates that the average inter-LATA rate in 1996 was $0.145 a minute; the PNR data show that residences paid an average of $0.176. Therefore, we estimate that total U.S. business long-distance traffic was about 150 percent of residential traffic in 1996.

18. Later, we show the results in certain dimensions for as many as twenty different states.

19. Long-distance carriers now offer discount plans with rates as low as nine to ten cents a minute, regardless of distance or time of day, from which they must pay three cents a minute in access charges.

20. We do not pursue this latter approach because, as discussed above, we know that business rates are already far below residential rates, largely because many large business customers use leased lines (special access) to bypass switched access charges at one or both ends of their calls.

21. Lewis Perl, "Social Welfare and Distributional Consequences of Cost-Based Telephone Pricing," paper prepared for the thirteenth annual Telecommunications Policy Research Conference, Va., 1985. The estimate of $76 is based on Perl's $48 estimate, inflated for changes in the Consumer Price Index.

22. See Affidavit of Robert Crandall and Leonard Waverman in "Application of Ameritech Michigan Pursuant to Section 271 of the Telecommunications Act of 1996 to Provide In-Region, Inter-LATA Services in Michigan, CC Docket No. 97–137" (Washington, May 20, 1997); and Jerry Hausman, "Taxation by Telecommunications Regulation," *Tax Policy and the Economy*, vol. 12 (1998), pp. 29–48, assumes that the marginal cost of long-distance is 25 percent of its price. Since the average price paid by consumers in the 1996 PNR sample was slightly more than seventeen cents, his assumption is very similar to ours.

23. The full effects, including the increases in producer surplus from additional long-distance calling, are shown in table 6-8.

24. Table 6-6 shows the estimated consumer gains from abandoning current universal service pricing policies. Therefore, the signs are negative for income groups that gain from these policies.

25. In 1996 residential inter-LATA rates averaged seventeen and a half cents a minute [PNR and Associates, *Bill Harvesting III* (Jenkintown, Pa., 1996)], and all inter-LATA rates averaged fourteen and a half cents a minute ("Affidavit of Robert E. Hall"). Assuming that business minutes are 150 percent of residential minutes, the average business inter-LATA rate would be twelve and a half cents a minute.

26. See Taylor, *Telecommunications Demand*, for a review of the limited number of studies of the demand for long-distance services in the business sector.

27. Robert W. Crandall, *After the Breakup: U.S. Telecommunications in a More Competitive Era* (Brookings, 1991).

28. Larger businesses use a variety of high-volume services and their own networks to avoid such charges.

29. We are indebted to David Newberry of Oxford University for suggesting this to us.

Chapter 7

1. The commission initially set these thresholds at tentative levels of $31 a month for residences and $51 a month for businesses. See Federal Communications Commission, "Report and Order in the Matter of Federal-State Joint Board on Universal Service, CC Docket 96–45," FCC 97–157, May 8, 1997, para. 267. In 1999, however, the commission changed direction somewhat, deciding that the threshold or "benchmark" should be based on some mark-up on the average national cost per line. FCC, "Seventh Report and Order and Thirteenth Order on Reconsideration in CC Docket 96–451, Fourth Report and Order in CC Docket 96–262 and Further Notice of Proposed Rulemaking," FCC 99–119, May 28, 1999.

2. See chapter 6 for a discussion of cost models.

3. 1996 Telecommunications Act, sec. 254b.

4. These charges are simply regulatory artifacts for converting the inefficient per minute access charges into per line charges. The subscriber line charge began immediately after the breakup of AT&T in 1984, while the presubscriber interexchange carrier charges were introduced much later in an effort to restructure rates without giving the overt appearance of increasing monthly residential rates.

5. It is not only difficult to estimate with precision the costs that current telephone companies incur in serving each subscriber, but it is impossible to predict how entrants might configure their networks with new technologies to serve these same customers.

6. FCC, "Ninth Report and Order and Eighteenth Order on Reconsideration, CC Docket 96–45," FCC 99–306, November 2, 1999.

7. Universal service taxes are currently levied on residential and business services. In our simulations, we assume that the taxes are levied only on residential services. If the taxes are levied on business services as well, the tax rate can be lower, but the economic distortions will be greater if business demand is more price sensitive than is residential demand.

8. Our revenue base for 1996 is approximately $60 billion for residential revenues. By comparison, the Census Bureau's estimate for all carriers offering residential local and long-distance service is $68 billion. Part of the difference lies in our exclusion of Alaska and Hawaii. The rest is attributable to the omission of CAPs and other carriers. Were the revenue base all business and residential service, including wireless, it would have been about $177 billion in 1996.

9. These rates are much higher than those envisioned by the FCC for several reasons. First, the FCC does not envision full rate rebalancing. Second, the FCC includes business and wireless services in its revenue base. Finally, the FCC does not discuss the intrastate taxes required for rate rebalancing.

10. According to the Census Bureau, *Annual Survey of Communications Services, 1996,* business customers accounted for 54 percent of all local and long-distance revenues in 1996.

11. See Lester D. Taylor, *Telecommunications Demand in Theory and Practice* (Dordrecht: Kluwer, 1994), chap. 8 and apps. 1 and 2 for a summary of the empirical literature on business demand for telephone services. Many of these studies conclude that business demand for services such as Centrex and WATS is price elastic. Preliminary research on cellular demand by one of the present authors suggests that the decision to purchase cellular service has about the same price elasticity as the demand for traditional long-distance services.

12. FCC, "Ninth Report and Order and Eighteenth Order on Reconsideration, CC Docket 96–45," FCC 99–306, November 2, 1999; and FCC, "Proposed First Quarter 2000 Universal Service Contribution Factor, CC Docket 96–45," DA 99–2780, December 10, 1999.

13. *Texas Office of Public Utility Counsel v. FCC,* 183 F.3d 393 (5th Cir. 1999).

14. See FCC, "Comments of the Coalition for Affordable Local and Long Distance Service (CALLS) in the matter of CC Dockets 94–1, 96–45, 99–249, and 96–262," November 12, 1999.

15. The most recent data are through the end of 1998. See FCC, Common Carrier Bureau, "Response to the Fourth CCB Survey on the State of Local Competition," June 2, 1999.

16. Mark Kastan and Dan Reingold, "Telecom Services—Local," Merrill Lynch, New York, June 3, 1999; and FCC, Common Carrier Bureau, *Local Competition* (Washington: August 1999), tables 3.1, 3.3.

17. These charges currently add $5.01 to the average residential subscriber's monthly bill. See William Rogerson and Evan Kwerel, "A Proposal for Universal Service and Access Reform," May 26, 1999. But the commission has been reluctant to move in this direction even when prompted by the industry coalition advancing the CALLS proposal (see note 14).

Chapter 8

1. Jeffrey K. MacKie-Mason and Hal R. Varian. "Economic FAQs about the Internet," in Lee W. McKnight and Joseph P. Bailey, eds., *Internet Economics* (MIT Press, 1997), pp. 27–62.

2. It may be possible to identify voice calls by their terminating address, but such a procedure would probably be defeated by frequent changing of addresses.

3. Internet usage is not measured or billed, complicating the pricing issues. One innovative method, Paris Metro Pricing (PMP), establishes two classes of service with a "first class" that has less congestion and a higher fee.

4. It is now possible for there to be two separate, simultaneous transmissions over the same subscriber loop—one providing voice calls and the other transmitting high-speed, advanced services—by digital subscriber-line (DSL) technology.

5. Robin Mason, "Internet Telephony and the International Accounting Rate System," *Telecommunications Policy*, vol. 22 (December 1998), pp. 931–44. See especially p. 939 for sources of cost estimates.

6. Jiong Gong and Padmanabhan Srinagesh, "The Economics of Layered Networks," in McKnight and Bailey, *Internet Economics*, p. 71.

7. The result has been to assign long-distance users very high (access) charges for connecting to the local switching network.

8. Martyne M. Hallgren and Alan K. McAdams, "A Model for Efficient Aggregation of Resources for Economic Public Goods on the Internet," in McKnight and Bailey, *Internet Economics*, p. 456.

9. Padmanabhan Srinagesh, "Internet Cost Structures and Interconnection Agreements," in McKnight and Bailey, *Internet Economics*, p. 129.

10. See the Robert Harris affidavit filed in opposition to the Worldcom-MCI merger. FCC, "First Affidavit of Robert G. Harris on Behalf of GTE Communications Corporation, CC Docket 97–211," March 13, 1998.

11. Srinagesh, "Internet Cost Structures and Interconnection Agreements," p. 142.

12. Hallgren and McAdams. "A Model for Efficient Aggregation of Resources," p. 456.

13. However, new technological developments are reducing congestion by caching intensely demanded content at servers close to the users.

14. For example, in November 1997, France Telecom announced a package of thirty hours of local usage for 100 francs a month, a rate that is apparently greater than long-run incremental cost.

15. MacKie-Mason and Varian, "Economic FAQs about the Internet," p. 29.

16. *www.nua.ie/surveys/how_many_online/index.html[January 11, 2000]*.

17. Network Wizards (http://www.isc.org/ds/WWW-9907/report.html [January 11, 2000]). While there were 43.2 million listed hosts as of January 1999, only 8.4 million of these responded to inquiries for information. Table 8-2 lists the number of hosts by country as of July 1998 (active and inactive).

18. National Telecommunications and Information Administration, *Falling Through the Net: Defining the Digital Divide* (Department of Commerce: July 1999), pp. 17, 85; and Eric C. Newburger, *Computer Use in the United States: October 1997,* P20–522 (U.S. Bureau of the Census, 1999).

19. National Telecommunications and Information Administration, *Falling through the Net,* p. 34.

20. OECD, *Communications Outlook 1999* (Paris, 1999) p. 86.

21. *www.internet.com* [August 8, 1999].

22. Since then, AOL has raised its price to $21.95 a month.

23. *Financial Times,* February 22, 1998.

24. See the Dell Computer website (*http://www.dell.com/us/en/gen/default.htm* [August 8, 1999]). For instance, a computer can be purchased for $959, including one year's Internet service, which would cost $239.40 if purchased separately.

25. *www.internetnews.com/isp-news* [July 15,1999].

26. This is based on the fact that 42 percent have computers; of these, about 72 percent have modems.

27. Paul N. Rappoport, Lester D. Taylor, and Donald J. Kridel, "An Econometric Study of the Demand for Access to the Internet," unpublished (November 1997); and Robert W. Crandall and Charles L. Jackson, "Eliminating Barriers to DSL Service," study undertaken for the United States Telephone Association (Washington, May 1998).

28. The act introduces subsidies for more advanced telecom services to schools, libraries, and rural medical facilities, but advanced services are not required for routine Internet connections or for e-mail.

29. It would be difficult to limit the subsidy to new subscribers because today's AOL subscriber could easily become tomorrow's MCI Internet subscriber in order to qualify for the subsidy.

30. Robert H. Anderson and others, *Universal Access to E-Mail: Feasibility and Societal Implications* (Washington: RAND, 1995), p. xiv.

31. An exception is Andy H. Barnett and David L. Kaserman, "The Simple Welfare Economics of Network Externalities and the Uneasy Case for Subscribership Subsidies," *Journal of Regulatory Economics*, vol. 13 (May 1998), pp. 245–54.

32. Rappoport, Taylor, and Kridel, "An Econometric Study of the Demand for Access to the Internet."

33. These points are made in Anderson and others, *Universal Access to E-Mail*.

34. This was a 1994 Study by EMMS cited in Anderson and others, *Universal Access to E-Mail*, p. 86.

35. *London Times*, March 1998.

36. The prices of computers are also higher in Europe than in the United States, suggesting to some that lower European penetration rates are mainly due to prices and income. See *International Herald Tribune*, March 19, 1998.

37. See Anderson and others, *Universal Access to E-Mail*, p. 88.

38. Anderson and others, *Universal Access to E-Mail*, p. 105.

39. Hal Varian, "Differential Pricing and Efficiency," *First Monday*, vol. 1 (August 5, 1996) (*http://www.firstmonday.dk/issues/issue2/different/index.html* [March 7, 2000]).

40. Support was $2.25 billion for schools and libraries and $400 million for other elements of the new program. FCC, "Third Quarter 1998. Universal Service Contribution Factors Revised and Approved, CC Docket 96–45," DA 98–1130, June 12, 1998. See FCC, "Proposed First Quarter 2000 Universal Service Contribution Factors, CC Docket 96–45," DA 99–2780, December 10, 1999.

41. In the event of excess demand, the FCC starts at the highest discount, funds all requests at that level, and then moves down the discount range.

42. 34 CFR 200.28. Not surprisingly, appeals have been launched by schools that were deemed urban (thus receiving lower discounts).

43. These funds can only be accessed by a school making a "technology plan" that is approved by the state education agency. That agency posts the plan, it is hoped, on the Internet, and the lowest bidder, subject to quality, receives the contract. As there may be more schools and libraries eligible than funds available, funding is on a first come, first served basis. Two commissioners, Harold Furchtgott-Roth and Michael Powell, question whether the FCC's May 28, 1999, increase in funding to $2.25 billion is in the public interest compared with the other components of universal service. See their separate statements: FCC, "Twelfth Order on Reconsideration in the matter of Federal State Joint Board on Universal Service, CC Docket No. 96–45," FCC 99–121, May 28, 1999.

44. The tax on any positive externality should be funded with a tax on a good or service whose demand is correlated with the willingness to pay for the externality. See Peter Diamond and James Mirrlees, "Optimal Taxation and Public Production II: Tax Rules," *American Economic Review*, vol. 61 (June 1971), part 1, pp. 261–78. It seems far fetched, however, to claim that one's willingness to pay for Internet subsidies or telecom subsidies for Internet connections is correlated with one's use of the telephone network. Rather, it is likely to be correlated with income or some other indicator of charitable contributions.

45. National Center for Education Statistics, *Issue Brief: Internet Access in Public Schools*, NCES 98–031, March 1998.

46. See FCC, "Statement of Chairman William E. Kennard on Funding for the Second Year of the Schools and Libraries and Rural Health Care Universal Support Mechanisms," May 27, 1999.

47. FCC, "Public Notice: Third Quarter 1998 Universal Service Contribution Factors Revised and Approved, CC Docket 96–45," DA 98–1130, June 12, 1998; and "Fifth Order on Reconsideration and Fourth Report and Order in CC Docket 96–45," FCC 98–120, June 22, 1998.

48. The FCC levied a tax of just 2.6 percent on a tax base of interstate and international revenues, including wireless revenues, to fund the program at an annual rate of $2 billion during the first quarter of 2000. See FCC, "Proposed First Quarter 2000 Universal Service Contribution Factors, CC Docket 96–45," DA 99–2780, December 10, 1999. Jerry Hausman obtains a much larger estimate of the welfare cost of the program in "Taxation by Telecommunications Regulation," *Tax Policy and the Economy*, vol.12 (1998) pp. 29–48.

Chapter 9

1. See Milton L. Mueller, *Universal Service: Competition, Interconnection, and Monopoly in the Making of the American Telephone System* (MIT Press and AEI Press, 1997), and chapter 1 in this volume.

2. See our discussion of EU policies and Canadian policy in chapter 1. Pressure is mounting in Australia for "rate rebalancing" because of the threat posed by new entrants, such as Optus, to the incumbent, Telstra.

3. See Andy H. Barnett and David. L. Kaserman, "The Simple Welfare Economics of Network Externalities and the Uneasy Case for Subscribership Subsidies," *Journal of Regulatory Economics*, vol.13 (May 1998), pp. 245–54.

4. We showed this in chapter 7.

5. For example, rural Appalachia and not Vail, Colorado.

6. In most other developed countries, motor fuel taxes are simply a source of general revenue to be used for various purposes.

7. Mark Kaplan and Daniel Reingold, "Telecom Services—Local," Merrill Lynch, New York, June 3, 1999.

8. Separate statement of Commissioner Furchtgott-Roth on "Proposed Second Quarter 1998 Universal Service Contribution Factors Announced in FCC CC Docket 96–45," February 27, 1998.

9. FCC, "Third Quarter 1998 Universal Service Contribution Factors Revised and Approved, CC Docket 96–45," DA 98–1130, June 12, 1998.

10. Of course, once long-distance rates have declined to a competitive level, these problems are much less onerous.

Index

195